A Soldier of the Legion

A Soldier of the Legion

An Englishman's Adventures Under the French Flag in Algeria and Tonquin

By

George Manington

Enhanced Media
2017

A Soldier of the Legion - An Englishman's Adventures Under the French Flag in Algeria and Tonquin by George Manington. First published in 1907. This edition published 2017 by Enhanced Media. All rights reserved.

Enhanced Media Publishing
Los Angeles, CA.

First Printing: 2017.

ISBN-13: 978-1545124475

ISBN-10: 1545124477

Contents

Dedication 6
Preface 7
CHAPTER I 8
CHAPTER II 25
CHAPTER III 36
CHAPTER IV 63
CHAPTER V 89
CHAPTER VI 109
CHAPTER VII 130
CHAPTER VIII 145

Dedication

To the memory of my comrades who fell in the forests of Yen-Thé and the jungles of Kai-Kinh, this work is dedicated.

Preface

Sitting at the terrace of a well-known café, on the main boulevard of the French capital, some time ago, I happened to glance down the columns of a Parisian newspaper, and was struck by a realistic account of the recent combat at El-Moungar.

After describing this action,—a long, arduous, but successful defence of a convoy of arms and ammunition by a handful of men from the Foreign Legion against the repeated attacks of more than a thousand fanatical Moorish horsemen,—the journalist expressed his admiration for the courage and disinterested devotion of which this corps has so often given proof.

The final phrase of his article can well serve as an excuse for, and introduction to, the present volume:—*Si quelque philosophe ouvrait un jour une chaire pour enseigner l'heroïsme et le dévouement, son cours pourrait se tenir tout entier dans la lecture des citations obtenues par la Légion Étrangère.*

G.M., HONG-KONG.

CHAPTER I

Most Englishmen, whose knowledge of the gay city of Paris is in the slightest degree superior to that of the ordinary summer tripper, are acquainted with the fine red stone building on the Boulevard St Germain, which is known as the Ministère de la Guerre, therefore it is unnecessary to give a lengthy description of this imposing edifice; above all, as its connection with the present history is of the shortest. It must, however, be explained why I, on the morning of the 26th February 1890, after pushing aside a big swing-door, found myself in the vestibule of this home of the supreme direction of one of the largest standing armies in the world, whose glorious traditions began on the field of Ivry, and amongst whose galaxy of leaders figure the personalities of Condé, Turenne, Carnot, Hoche, Bonaparte, Canrobert and MacMahon.

I chanced one evening, after I had been living for the past two years in the French capital, whilst in the company of several army officers, to meet an Austrian gentleman, of old lineage and great wealth, who entertained us with the recital of his experiences during the Tonquin campaign of 1883-85. Owing to an affaire de cœur, he had enlisted in the Foreign Legion, had risen to the rank of sergeant-major, was twice wounded, and had been decorated with the *médaille militaire* for bravery in action.

This narrative so excited my imagination and desire for adventure that I fell into slumber that night only after having decided on taking a similar course, in the hope of warring in strange lands and seeing life out of the rut.

I should here say, before going further, that owing to the action so suddenly decided upon, I was often in the future to undergo suffering and privation; yet never once during the five years of my service did I regret the step taken and wish it retraced.

The next morning I put my project into execution, and, as aforesaid, went to the fountain-head for information. Perhaps the officials may have had serious doubts as to whether I was in my right mind; and there was some excuse for them, for it is not every day that an individual comes to the Ministère, and in a matter-of-fact manner asks to enlist, in just such a way as one might ask for a room at an hotel. Whatever their thoughts may have been, they were exceedingly obliging, and informed me that I must go to the Rue St Dominique, the central recruiting office, and obtain all the necessary information.

Somewhat disappointed at the delay, I started off at once for the destination they had indicated to me, which is near to the famous Hôtel des Invalides, and half an hour later found myself in a room which bore a strong resemblance to the booking-office of a London railway station. There were wooden benches round three sides of it, and five wickets in the wall on the fourth. Facing the entrance and in the corner of the room was a door, on which was painted in white letters, "Bureau du Commandant de Recrutement"; and in the other corner, on the same side, was another exit, leading to the room where, as I afterwards learnt, the medical examination of future recruits took place. Upon the whitewashed walls were several notices all bearing the same heading, "République Française—Liberté, Égalité, Fraternité," and containing instructions to conscripts as to the time and place at which they must present themselves for enlistment.

It is hardly necessary to state that military service is compulsory in France. There were about thirty men in the room, some sitting alone, or in pairs, on the benches, others standing in groups. They were of all classes of society, if one could judge by their costumes, and the conversations which were going on were little above a whisper. A sort of timid expectancy seemed to reign supreme.

Little or no attention was paid to my entrance, so I had time to take things in. Espying over one of the wickets the words, "Engagements Volontaires," I walked up to it, and attracted the attention of a sergeant of the line who was in the office writing in a big ledger. When I had stated my object he stared very hard at me, and, having taken my name, told me to wait until called for.

I went over and sat on one of the benches, from which could be seen all that was going on in the room, and amused myself by examining the different types present, speculating, meanwhile, on the social status of each and the wherefore of their presence.

There were many who were mere lads, the eldest of whom could not have been more than nineteen. From scraps of their conversation which reached me it was evident that they were volunteers who came to offer their services before the time had arrived for their incorporation, which is generally between the ages of twenty and twenty-one years. They were drawn from all classes, and were attired in anything from the silk hat and blue velvet-collared sacque coat of the well-to-do bourgeois to the dark cotton blouse and casquette so popular on the boulevards extérieurs. Seated in one corner were two young men who bore the outward stamp of respectability. These, I afterwards learnt, were in quest of the medical certificate which would allow them to enter the Military Academy of St Cyr, which, like our college at Sandhurst, is a school for army officers.

My attention was next drawn to a group of six or seven individuals who were standing in a circle round one, whose rotund face and short red hair could be seen above their heads. They were all men of from twenty to thirty years of age. Several of them were neat and clean in appearance, and seemed to be of the artisan class, but there were others in a decidedly "down-at-heel" condition. The red-headed man was evidently a wit in his way, if one could judge by the smiles and low laughter which greeted his frequent sallies; and I was regretting that I could not catch the meaning of his words, being too far away for that, when by chance our eyes met; and after making his way out of the group, he came across the room, sat beside me, and opened the conversation with a polite "Bonjour, Monsieur!"—to which I responded with equal urbanity.

"Excuse me," said my interlocutor, "but you are not a Frenchman, are you?"

"No; I am an Englishman."

Then desirous, no doubt, of excusing his seeming indiscretion, he continued:

"I asked you that question because I am myself a stranger—a Swiss—and from your appearance I thought you might be here with a similar intention to my own: that of enlisting in the Foreign Legion. Am I right?"

"Yes," I answered, having no reason to conceal the object of my presence there, and, besides, the looks of the man rather pleased me. He was evidently a frank-speaking, good-tempered fellow, and his clean-shaven face and neat exterior indicated a certain respectability. I took him for an actor or a gentleman's valet. Knowing that I should be likely to meet and mix with all sorts and conditions of men in the road I had chosen, on taking my decision I had determined to accept things as they were without complaint, so long as the life would bring me new experiences which I could not hope to encounter in the ordinary stay-at-home, humdrum existence.

"Well," he continued, "it appears that we have both chosen the same route. I hope we shall be in the same regiment."

"The same regiment!" I exclaimed in surprise, "I thought there was only one Legion."

"Formerly it was so," he replied; "but that fellow over there—a German, who is going to enlist for a second time—tells me that about five years ago the old Legion was formed into two corps, which go by the name of the 1st and 2nd Régiments Étrangers."

I looked in the direction he indicated, and saw a tall man of about thirty, whose stalwart form and straight shoulders betokened the soldier. He was reading one of the bills on the walls. This information interested me immensely, and I was just thinking of how I could best approach this individual with the view of obtaining fresh details, when the door of the Commandant's office opened suddenly and a non-commissioned officer appeared, and, to my consternation, shouted out my name. Instinctively I rose and answered "Present," just as if I were answering to a call-over at school, all the other occupants of the room eyeing me curiously as I did so.

In response to a gesture from the sergeant I stepped across, entered the office, and found myself in the presence of a gentleman in the uniform of a major of the line, who was seated at a big table covered with papers and text-books. He was a red-faced man of about forty, with short-cropped grey hair and a heavy moustache of the same tint. The eyes that looked into mine had a kindly light in them, which belied the somewhat brusque manner of their owner.

I uncovered as I entered the room, and saluted him with the stereotyped "Bonjour, Monsieur!" to which he nodded a response, and, without further preamble, said:

"So you are desirous of enlisting in one of the Régiments Étrangers?"

"Yes, sir," I replied.

"Since when have you come to that decision?"

This unexpected question rather nonplussed me, but regaining my composure I answered with apparent coolness:

"Oh! since yesterday."

He smiled, and then said, to my astonishment and anger:

"Eh *bien*! you are a fool, my friend. Ah! that hurts you, doesn't it?" (I had flushed at his observation). "Sure proof that stern discipline would not suit you," he continued. Then in a softened and more kindly tone he rattled along so quickly that there was no chance of putting in a word:

"*Sacré bleu*! The Legion—why, you don't know what it is. Well, I will tell you—hard work—hard knocks—hard discipline, and no thanks. And how does it end? Your throat cut by some thieving Arab if you have luck; if not, wounded, and then his women make sausage meat of you. In Tonquin the same sort of thing—only worse, with fever and sunstroke into the bargain. A bad business! yes, a bad business!" Then his voice took quite a paternal tone, and he continued: "You look like a gentleman—you are one, I'm sure. Mind you, I don't mean to say there are not others over there—there are many—poor fellows! Your family, too!—think of them—such a sudden decision. Sapristi! and all for some trifling *bêtise, sans doute*. A petticoat, I'll swear—don't deny it—I have been young also—a faithless sweetheart—Pish! There are a thousand others who would be delighted to console you. No! No! A good dinner, the Moulin Rouge, and to-morrow you will be cured, sacré bleu!" He laughed, and added: "Try that; and if to-morrow you still feel the cravings for a military career, well, come and see me."

Disappointed and somewhat resentful, for at the time I did not appreciate the kindly intention which underlay the advice he had given me, and imagined that I had been treated with undue contempt and familiarity, I replied:

"Tomorrow I shall return, sir!"

He laughed again good-naturedly, and said:

"Well, well, we shall see;" at which I bowed and left the room.

The outer office was silent and deserted, for it was the luncheon hour. I was annoyed at this, having counted on obtaining more information from the other men who had come to join. However, recognising the inutility of waiting there, I proceeded to my usual restaurant in a very disappointed state of mind, though in no way turned from my determination.

At an early hour the next morning I returned to the Rue St Dominique. The major, my friend of the day before, received me with many deprecatory remarks concerning my persistence; but seeing that they were evidently lost on me, he carefully perused my passport, which I had been particular to bring with me, and I was passed on to the doctor for examination. *"Bon pour le service,"* ran the verdict given, and I was then signed on for a period of five years.

After much waiting a *feuille de route*, a railway requisition for Marseilles, and the sum of three francs for expenses, were given me. The sergeant-major who handed them to me was kind enough to mention that should I fail to put in an appearance at my destination within the next forty-eight hours, I would be considered a deserter, and treated as such. I left Paris that evening from the "Gare de Lyons," and arrived at Marseilles about twenty-four hours afterwards.

At this stage of my story it is right to give a short historical description of the corps in which I had enlisted, and concerning which so many errors have been written, and so many delusions exist.

The Foreign Legion first came into existence in the early 'thirties of the last century. It was composed chiefly of foreign adventurers who had flocked to Algeria at the time of the French invasion of that country. Shortly after its formation it acquired a reputation for courage and recklessness which has never been allowed to die, and of which its officers and Legionaries are proud to a fault.

Since its creation it has served with honour and distinction in nearly every campaign undertaken by France. In Algeria, the Crimea, Mexico, Tonquin, Formosa and Madagascar the Legion was to the fore. The Legionaries, led by their colonel, MacMahon, the future Marshal and President of the Republic, were the first to scale the breach and enter the city of Constantine on the 12th October, 1837, after an hour's bloody hand-to-hand conflict, during which half of their effective were blown sky-high by a mine. They shared the same honours with the Zouaves at the Malakoff under Canrobert, and the defence of Tuayen-Quang (Tonquin), by eight hundred of this corps under Commandant Dominé, during nearly four months of continual sap and assault, against an army of twelve thousand well-drilled Chinese troops, is one of the finest feats of arms in modern times. In France the blood of this fine corps has flowed like water. In the winter of 1870, when it was decided by France's generals that Orleans should be evacuated, two battalions of the Legion, which had just arrived from Africa, were entrusted with the defence of the suburbs of the town; thereby covering the retreat of the main army. During six hours they held back the Prussian forces, and were practically annihilated, for they lost seventy-five per cent. of their total strength in killed or wounded, and it was never possible for them to figure again as a corps of any importance in the campaign which followed; but they saved the Army of the Loire, for the Prussians suffered such terrible losses, and were so completely exhausted by their repeated efforts, that all immediate pursuit was out of the question.

The corps also holds a record for having had as officers men who eventually became some of the most famous commanders of modern France; MacMahon, Canrobert, Chanzy, De Négrier, Servière, and the ill-advised but brave and romantic Villebois de Mareuil were amongst the number. Originally, in addition to the many adventurers, whom military instincts, hopes of plunder, and desire for excitement had led to enlist, there were certainly a good many scallywags, perhaps criminals; but to-day there are few, if any. Police methods have changed considerably since the beginning of the last century, and a fugitive from justice would be a fool indeed if he thought he could evade punishment by joining the ranks of a "Régiment Étranger"; for by so doing he would be thrusting his head into the noose, even had he been able to procure papers affording him a change of identity to enlist with, for nearly every one at one time or another has had their photograph taken, and it is no easy matter to cheat the camera, neither is it possible to evade the searching tests of the anthropometric system.

The Legion, or rather the two Foreign Regiments of to-day, are composed of deserters from other armies—of these the Germans are in the majority—men out of work who don't wish to starve, and who can't beg; scallywags, i.e. those men who have gambled or squandered their money and can't work; officers who have been forced to resign owing to some private scandal; and the hundred other culprits and victims of the social conventions of to-day, the description of whose grievances, or the peccadilloes which brought about their presence in the corps, would require a volume in itself. Besides all these, strange as it may seem to the calm, well-balanced mind of the properly educated majority of respectable society, there is a comparatively great number of seekers after adventure who enlist, some of whom actually possess an income of their own, and are often too generous with it, for, much to the annoyance of the sergeant for the week who controls the peregrinations of the men punished with pack-drill, wine is cheap and good in Algeria. Be they what they may when they join, deserter, unemployed, ex-officer, gambler, defrocked priest, member of a reigning family (for I knew of two such during my service), taken collectively they are all Legionaries and *bons camarades* once under the flag, for, with but few exceptions, they possess at least one, and sometimes many good traits of character, and together they form one of the smartest and bravest infantry corps in the world.

The Legion originally possessed its own artillery and engineers, but these were abolished in the 'fifties, and it became exclusively an infantry corps. In 1885 it was formed into two regiments of four battalions each, and in 1895 the effective of each corps was increased by a battalion.

I arrived in Marseilles about nine o'clock in the evening, and having addressed myself to a non-commissioned officer who was on the platform, I was conducted by him to the depot, known as the "Incurables," and lodged for the night. This was my first experience of a military bed and barracks, and it must be confessed that I was not favourably impressed by their cleanliness, or rather their want of it. Here I met again my friend of the recruiting office, and six other volunteers for the Foreign Regiments, and learnt from him that his name was Balden, and that, like myself, he had been placed in the first of these two corps. He had arrived the day before, and told me that we should leave for Oran on the morrow by the steamer Abd-el-Kader.

The next morning, 1st March, 1890, we awoke for the first time to the note of the bugle sounding the réveil; and after a wash and brush up in the lavatory, came back to the barrack-room, where I had slept, to partake of the usual morning meal of the French soldier—a mug of sweetened black coffee and a slice of bread.

The room in which we had passed the night was, together with the furniture it contained, of the regulation type, to be met with in the barracks of most Continental armies. It was about 75 feet long, and 20 broad; there was a door in the middle of each of the longest sides, and three windows at either end. It contained twenty-four cots, six on either side of the doors. These beds consist of two iron trestles, with three pine planks laid over them. A straw mattress, a bolster, a brown blanket, and two coarse sheets complete the outfit. Along both sides of the room is a shelf upon which each French soldier arranges his neatly-folded kit, which must be placed just above the bed he is occupying. From several hooks fixed underneath the shelf, are suspended the water-bottles, belts, cartridge cases, bayonets, and canvas wallets of the men. These must, of course, be arranged in a similar and regulation manner by each one. In the middle of the room, between the two doors, is the gun-rack in which all the rifles of the occupants are placed. Between the rack and the window, at either end of the room, is a plain wooden table with benches; it is at this that the meals are taken. Just over every cot is suspended, from a nail in the edge of the shelf, a card bearing the name, number and grade of the man who occupies it. The room lodges two squads, each of which is under the orders of a corporal; the "non-coms" being responsible for the maintenance of order and cleanliness. Generally the rooms in French barracks present a very clean and smart appearance. Such was not the case with the one we slept in at Marseilles; but this can easily be accounted for by the fact that it was used by a succession of passing recruits, who possessed no kit and no knowledge of their duties, and who occupied it for two or three days at a time, or for a night only.

At nine that morning I was detailed off by a sergeant to go with another man and fetch the meal for the room. We brought it back from the cook-house in a sort of big wooden tray with a handle at each end. The repast consisted of a loaf weighing about one pound and a half—the day's ration of bread—and a tin pannikin full to the brim with stewed white beans, a piece of boiled beef and two boiled potatoes, for each recruit. I must say that the food did not appeal to me at the time, but it was good and clean, and exercise and a healthy appetite soon made it palatable.

Food in the French army varies somewhat in its composition—that is to say, lentils or rice are sometimes substituted for beans, pork or mutton for beef; but the mode of cooking was the same at each meal, and it was only on such grand occasions as the 14th July or New Year's Day that roast meat was given. This, however, only applies to the troops in France or Algeria, for those in the Colonies receive a much greater variety of diet. I have heard also, since leaving the army, that considerable change has taken place in this respect, and that some of the regiments of the line are now quite famous for their menus.

At eleven we were called down to the barrack-yard and lined up. Here we were joined by another detachment in civilian clothes; these were recruits for the French regiments in Algeria, the "Zouaves" and "Chasseurs d'Afrique." The roll was called, and we were afterwards marched down to the "Vieux Port" and embarked on the steamer before-mentioned, which proceeded to sea shortly afterwards.

We arrived in Oran about six in the evening on the following day, and were immediately conducted to the barracks, where we found a preceding detachment awaiting our arrival to proceed to the interior. Of this Algerian city I saw little or nothing on this occasion, as my stay consisted of a few hours only, and during the whole time we had to remain in the barracks.

The next morning sixteen of us left by an early train for the town of Sidi-bel-Abbes, at which is the depot of the 1st Régiment Étranger, and we arrived at our destination about five o'clock in the evening. I felt some emotion as I marched with my companions through the gates into the barrack-yard, whilst the sentry and the men on duty standing about outside the guard-room eyed us with evident curiosity; and some of the latter made audibly rude remarks concerning our unsoldierlike appearance, and the amount of licking into shape we would require. The quadrangle, which was about 100 yards long by 80 broad, was surrounded on three sides by two-storied buildings. To the right and left these consisted of barrack-rooms and companies' offices on each floor; but on the third side, facing the gate, the building contained the infirmary, canteen, store-rooms, armoury and workshops of the regiment. No sooner had we been halted than we were surrounded, but at a respectful distance, by hundreds of soldiers in all sorts of costumes—fatigue, guard, undress and walking-out order—for the "non-coms" who had conducted us from the station threatened with dire pains and penalties all those who should approach too close. Chaffing queries in every European language were thrown at us, of which I came in for a good share, as, owing to my being the tallest present, I was the Number One, right-hand man of the detachment. One onlooker politely suggested that I had joined because the feeding of such a big specimen was too great an expense to my family. Unaccustomed to so much attention, I was somewhat annoyed by our reception, although outwardly preserving a cool demeanour; and I was greatly relieved when a sergeant-major appeared on the scene and called up several men from the guard-room to disperse the crowd. Our names were then called over, and we were conducted to a room in the barracks where we passed the night. On the morrow we were examined by the regimental doctor, and were given a regimental number. This is done for every soldier in the French army, and this number is stamped on every article of clothing and piece of kit he possesses.

The same day we were conducted to the Depot Camp, which lies just outside the town walls; for it is here that the recruits are kept for about six months until they are sufficiently drilled and disciplined to be drafted into the battalions.

At this time the 1st and 2nd Battalions of the regiment were in Tonquin, and the 3rd and 4th at Bel-Abbes, with detachments at Mecheria, Ain-Sefra, and in other smaller garrisons towards the south.

Here I was taken to the squad in which I had been placed, and handed over to the corporal who commanded it.

This "non-com" was an Alsatian, whose rough and rude exterior concealed a certain good-heartedness. Judging by appearances, I thought I had fallen into the hands of a brute, but soon discovered that notwithstanding the invectives and threats with which his mouth was for ever full, he was not a "bad sort," his bark being worse than his bite. His name was Hirschler, and he came from Strassburg. He possessed a pet grievance against the Government because Prussians were allowed to enlist in the regiment; and he hated the men of this race most heartily, for which there was some excuse, his father and mother having been killed by a shell during the bombardment of his native city in 1870.

He conducted me to the tent in which I was to lodge, pointed out my place, and went with me to the stores to draw a straw mattress, sleeping-sack, holster and a blanket. This done, he showed me how to fold them up and to dispose my kit.

This tent, like the others in the camp, was of the ordinary bell-shaped pattern. Round it a small trench is dug to prevent the rain from coming in. The floor is of beaten earth, and is about 6 inches higher than the ground outside of it. It usually gives shelter to eight men. During the day the mattresses are doubled up and placed round the interior close to the flies, which are then lifted so as to secure ventilation.

The blankets and sleeping-sacks are folded neatly and placed on the top of the bedding. About 6 feet from the ground is a circular board, and through the centre of this the pole of the tent passes; thus serving as a shelf on which the pannikins, tin cups, spoons, forks and knives of the men are kept. Underneath this shelf are hooks on which the rifles, belts and water-bottles are hung. Each man's knapsack is placed flat on the ground to the right of his bed, and his kit, which must be well folded, is placed upon it. The inside of the tents is kept very clean and tidy, and presents quite a smart appearance. This particular one contained seven occupants, including the corporal. The camp, which sheltered from five to six hundred men, was situated in a grove of laurel and eucalyptus trees; and during the spring and summer it presented a very picturesque and sylvan appearance. The weather was still very cold, and my first experience of outdoor life was rather a trying one. The winter of 1890 was exceptionally severe, as may be judged by the fact that on the morning of the 9th March I awoke to find the tent I was in covered with snow an almost unprecedented occurrence in Algeria.

During the first few days of my service I, together with the last batch of recruits, was drilled in camp each day. When we had sufficiently mastered the art of forming fours, marching and halting at the word of command, we were allowed to go out with the other companies to morning exercise on the parade ground outside the main gate of the town.

Sidi-bel-Abbes, like many French towns built in Algeria since the conquest of that country, is surrounded by a loopholed wall and ditch, with one or several gates on each side of it. I had been drilled at school, and found this of great help to me, so far as squad and section movements were concerned; but I had never handled a gun, and had rather a hard time learning the rifle and bayonet exercise, for the early mornings were very cold during the first six weeks, and my fingers would get so numbed that each time I touched the steel of my weapon it seemed to burn them to the bone. During the frequent intervals for rest the recruits of each squad would run round their stacked rifles, swinging their arms the while—like the cabmen on the ranks at home—to restore the circulation; and they would keep this up until the bugle sounded the "fall in" again.

However, when the weather became warmer and we "shaped" better, I rather enjoyed these three hours every morning; the first two of which were devoted to squad and section drill under the order of the "non-coms," and the last one to company and battalion movements directed by the officers.

At 9 a.m. we would march through the town back to camp, with the drum and fife band at our head. At 9.30 the first meal was served out. At 10 the companies assembled to hear the daily "report" read; and from 10.30 to 4 p.m. the time was taken up by gymnasium classes, fencing lessons, and the lectures and explanations given by the sergeants on duty, of the different text-books.

The whole day of Wednesday in each week was occupied by route-marching, and the afternoon of Friday by shooting on the range. The evening meal was at 4.30, and afterwards all men not on duty or the defaulters' book could go out till the retraite, which was at 8.45. Roll call was sounded at 9, and "lights out" at 10 p.m.

The life, though somewhat hard for a recruit, is not so bad as one might imagine. Discipline is always somewhat irksome at first, but one gets used to it. Some of the "non-coms" were objectionable, and seemed to delight in getting the men into trouble; but they were exceptions, and I managed to keep clear of them, thanks to my efforts to do my best, and a certain amount of goodwill. The corps maintained a great reputation for smartness, and a very searching kit inspection took place every Saturday afternoon. It was then that the private whose accoutrements were dirty, or whose linen was unwashed, got into serious trouble.

In the barracks there were lavatories, a washhouse, bath-room and an abundant supply of water; in the camp a stream which ran through it served the same purposes. With a little trouble a man could keep himself and his outfit in a state of cleanliness, and it was his own fault if he did not.

Much has been said concerning the iron discipline which reigns supreme in the Legion, but whilst serving with the corps I never suffered any real inconvenience from it: unless a punishment of "two days to barracks" can be considered of much account. It was well merited, for, through sheer carelessness, or perhaps because I wanted to get out a little sooner, I forgot that I was orderly man for the day, and left all the tin platters in the room after the evening meal was finished, instead of taking them down to the cook-house.

A regiment of men is not like a girls' school, and it is impossible to maintain discipline in a corps composed, as mine was, of so many "hard cases" unless a certain amount of severity is used.

In nearly all instances when prolonged punishments of "cells" and pack-drill were inflicted the offences originated through drunkenness; and the same is the truth for nine out of every ten cases in which court-martials were necessary.

Drink is the curse of all armies, and of the French one in particular. Wine is cheap, and, what is worse, absinthe is also; and the abuse of this stimulant is responsible for most of the individual cases of military crime in Algeria. Therefore the authorities are perfectly justified in using the severest methods to restrict and discourage the use of it.

About a fortnight after my arrival I was sitting one evening in my tent engrossed in the cleaning of my rifle, when the flap was lifted, and another private came in who did not belong to my squad. He was tall, fair, wore a heavy moustache, and presented a very erect and soldier-like appearance. He came straight up to me, and said in my own tongue:

"You are the Englishman, are you not?"

"Yes," I replied, much surprised at being thus addressed by a man I had never seen in my life before. "Who are you?"

"My name is Knox," he answered; "I joined last week at Calais. I am English too—or rather Scotch," he added with a laugh. "Having heard of you from some fellows in my tent, I have come over to look you up."

Really pleased to meet another Briton, I proposed an adjournment to the canteen, where we could talk at our ease. He acquiesced, and I proceeded to put the breech-bolt of my rifle together again. As I was doing so he picked up my gun, and after squinting down the barrel to see if it were clean, buckled the leather sling on again, for I had taken it off before starting operations, as one is instructed to do. He manipulated the weapon in such a "know-all-about-it" manner that I could not help observing:

"This is not the first time you've handled a rifle, Knox."

"You are right," he replied with a smile; "I was six years in the British army."

He handed me my gun, which, after adjusting the breech-bolt, I hung up on its hook. We then went over to the little wooden canteen, and over a pint of Algerian wine we exchanged confidences. He told me that he was from Edinburgh, had failed to get into Sandhurst, and "listed" as a private in an infantry regiment. He served in India with his corps, rose to the rank of sergeant and was broken after a "drunk"; was again promoted, and was in charge of a military telegraph station in Burmah during the last campaign. Tired of the service, he had "bought out," and returned to Scotland. Once home he had gone on a series of "busts," which had so disgusted his people that they had refused to come to his aid when he had run through all he possessed.

Almost devoid of resources, and having heard of the Legion, he went over to Calais and enlisted. He told me that he had the firm intention of turning over a new leaf and of doing his utmost to obtain a commission in his new corps, and I have no doubt, considering his previous experience, that he would have succeeded. Unfortunately, his career was cut short in a most untoward manner, much to my grief, an account of which is given in its proper place in this narrative.

Knox and I soon became fast friends. His knowledge of the calling was a great aid to me, and he was always glad to help by giving me "tips," which, small though they might seem, were of great assistance and often kept me from getting into trouble. On evenings and Sundays we passed all our spare time together, going for walks in the town, or outside of it.

We often visited the Arab quarter, which is the great curiosity of all Algerian towns. Together we would enjoy a dish of kus-kus, a slice of braised mutton, or a plateful of fresh dates, in a Moorish tavern; or sit over small cups of thick coffee and listen to a native story-teller, or watch the Moukirs dance in an Arab café.

On Sundays we went further afield, and took long walks through the vineyards, during which we would talk of home and our people, and speculate on what they might be doing.

When the warm weather had set in we would go out a few miles, on the road to Ain-Sefra and the desert, to a cluster of big olive trees—our favourite spot. We would lie down on the grass in the shade and talk over our chances of seeing active service, either in Tonquin or on the frontier of Morocco, until, tired of doing so, we would lapse into silence and, stretched flat on our backs, stare up at the patches of light blue sky visible between the green foliage, or at the ascending smoke of our cigarettes as it faded into space. Sometimes the soft warmth of the Algerian spring, the drone of the bees, and the monotonous chirp of the big grasshoppers would seduce us into a siesta, from which we awoke to watch with lazy eyes, which blinked at the strong sunlight, the veiled women coming from a spring near by, as with easy and graceful carriage they balanced on their heads the big earthenware pitchers full to the brim with water; or a long line of camels, laden with fresh dates and figs, striding along in their ungainly way towards the town, the silence broken only by the dull, shuffling sound made by their hoofs in the dust, or an occasional "Arawa!" from their white-clad Arab conductors.

During the month of May we made the acquaintance of a private whose name was Daly. He was an American, and an artist of no mean talent. He had studied painting in Paris, and was for some time, I believe, in the studio of Gérôme. Daly was a man of about five-and-twenty, under the average height, and of refined and pleasant manners. He had joined, he told me, after a run of very bad luck at Monte Carlo, where he had lost all the money allowed him by his father to defray his expenses during his period of study in France.

Although he had already been more than a year in the regiment when I met him, he had never handled a rifle. Since he had joined he had done nothing but paint the portraits and decorate the quarters of the officers. He willingly accompanied Knox and myself in our excursions, and shared our small pleasures, and we found him a most entertaining companion. He possessed the smallest feet I have ever seen on a man; and we would often chaff him about this trait, which was the despair of the regimental "corporal shoemaker," who was forced to make special boots for him, for the stores contained no fit for such diminutive extremities. I lost touch with him when I left Algeria, and have never heard of him since. I trust, however, that he continued an artist till the end of his military career, and that he is now enjoying the success his talent deserves somewhere in "God's country," as he used to call his native land.

Although I have only spoken of my intimates, Knox and Daly, I was soon on good terms with all the other men in my company whom I came in contact with, and the fact that I could converse in the languages most in use was of great help to me in maintaining good relations with them.

About sixty per cent of the Legionaries belong to Latin or French-speaking races; of these the Belgians, Swiss, and the majority of the Alsatians use that language, and the Italians and Spaniards very soon acquire it; but it was the rapidity with which the German and Austrian recruits gained a colloquial knowledge of it that surprised me. I attribute this to the fact that their education was generally of a higher standard than that possessed by the men of other nationalities.

About the middle of July, together with a batch of other recruits whose primary training had been found satisfactory by a board of examining officers, I was drafted into the 1st Company of the 3rd Battalion, which was lodged in the barracks.

On our arrival in our new quarters we were subjected to the usual series of practical jokes invented for the special benefit of "Johnny Raw," or "Le Bleu," as "Dumanet" calls the recruit. These pranks are of various descriptions, one of the most favourite being that of arranging a man's cot in such a manner that by pulling on the supports at the foot of it, it collapses, and its occupant slides out with all his bedding and kit on top of him.

Mock courts-martial by candle-light are also held on offenders who have broken the unwritten law of the barrack-room. The culprit is always found guilty, but generally escapes with a fine, consisting of a few litres of cheap wine, which is drunk by his room-mates, and of which he is invited to partake.

I never saw any real malice brought to bear in these jokes, and any one possessing a reasonable amount of good-humour can pass the ordeal, and even laugh at one's own occasional discomfiture.

The military education of the men in the battalion is a very serious matter, and is carried much further than at the depot. Particular care is given and a considerable amount of time devoted to perfecting the men in shooting and in training them for route-marching.

Good shots are encouraged by the distribution of badges placed on the sleeves, silver chains to be worn across the tunic, and watches of the same metal.

When I was drafted into the battalion, the troops were still using the rifle, model 1874—better known as the "Fusil Gras," the calibre and trajectory of which closely resembled those of the old Martini of the British army. This weapon was on the side-bolt principle, and its mechanism was so strong and simple that in the event of it becoming hard to manipulate owing to constant tiring the breech-bolt could be slipped out and cleansed of black powder grit in a few seconds by washing it in a puddle, or by pouring a little water over it. I have seen this done on several occasions in Tonquin when there had been hard shooting, for during the first year I was out there we still retained this weapon. When using the rifle, however, one had to be careful not to shoot with a loose shoulder, for its "kick" was tremendous; and I have sometimes seen a black eye or a bleeding nose the reward of those who neglected these precautions. The bayonet of this arm was of the sword pattern, with a blade about 2 feet long.

The system of training the infantrymen to perform long marches is an excellent one in the French army, and I have read the opinions of English military experts who declared that they are second to none in speed and endurance. Each Wednesday was devoted to this useful branch of military art.

The recruits start on their first march with their rifle and side arms only, and cover a distance of about 20 kilomètres—that is, about 12½ miles.

This distance is gradually increased, as is also the weight carried, until, a man loaded with all his kit, rifle and bayonet, reserve food for two days, a blanket, an entrenching tool and 120 rounds of ammunition, which represent a total weight of about 50 pounds, can perform a march of 45 kilomètres—that is, about 28 miles—in ten hours with ease. This space of time includes a rest of ten minutes in each hour whilst marching, and a halt of an hour for a meal. Deducting the time lost during the halts, the average speed is about 3½ miles an hour. In many cases during forced marches much better work is done, but the results given above are what the French infantryman who has been nine months with the colours can do with ease; and he maintains this standard during the remainder of his service, thanks to the continual training he undergoes. The men in each battalion of the Legion are very proud of the capabilities of their unit in this respect, and when called upon by their officers will make every effort to break records of forced marches made by other corps.

On the return to barracks after the march the non-commissioned officers of each company inspect the men's feet, and instruct their subordinates in the proper manner of treating blisters or chafes. I have myself seen an example when the results of this excellent system of training to resist fatigue has been of most signal service. As this incident is described in detail in a later chapter, I may simply mention that in January, 1892, a small relief column, of which I was a unit, performed a forced march of about 52 kilomètres,—or 32 miles—in eight hours.

This may not seem an extraordinary performance for Europe, but it must be borne in mind that it was done in the tropics, and that the road—if a path about a foot wide can be so called—ran through dense jungle and forest, or over slippery rocks, and that part of the distance was covered at night. In England the men are trained to route-marching during the summer and autumn only, which is due, no doubt, to the inclement weather of our winter and spring months; but in France and Algeria the troops are thus exercised right through the year. Whilst marching outside the towns the troops are allowed to smoke and sing.

All these military ditties, some of which date back in their origin to the early part of the eighteenth century, possess a swinging chorus, which is taken up by the whole column, with a surprisingly encouraging effect on the dust-stained, tired men, who, towards the end of a long day's tramp, are "swallowing the last kilomètre" with weary legs and aching loins.

It is of interest to note that the majority of French soldiers wear no socks when route-marching; this is owing to the fact that they generally chafe the feet of the walker. Some of the men wrap their feet in a triangular piece of linen which they call a chaussette russe; but in most cases nothing at all is worn inside the boot. Personally, I have found the last system the best conducive to comfort when a long distance has to be covered; but care must be taken that the boots worn fit well at the heel, ankle and instep, so that the foot does not slip about in them. They should be broad across the toes, and about half an inch longer than the foot itself; and, most important of all, should be so well greased that the leather of the uppers is as supple as india-rubber. Tallow is as good as anything for this purpose, but in Tonquin I found castor-oil—which is cheap and plentiful in the colony—a most excellent substitute.

CHAPTER II

Time flies apace when one is engrossed in mastering a new profession or calling, and I could with difficulty realise that only six short months separated me from my old life and complete ignorance of all things military, as, on one bright, hot morning in August, I stood at ease as the front rank man in No. 2 file of my company, which had mustered with all the strength of the regiment, and glanced at the serried ranks of the men of my corps, formed up on three sides of a square, round the barrack-yard. In the centre of this hollow square of men was the band of the regiment, and the detachment of sappers.

A few paces behind these were the colours, carried by a subaltern, and flanked by their guard with bayonets fixed. In front of the band and facing the barrack gates, which were in the centre and open side of the square, was Colonel Barbery, our commanding officer, mounted on a white Arab stallion with streaming mane and tail.

Our chief, if one could judge by the anxious glances he threw at his men and the repeated tugs he gave to his heavy white moustache, was impatient and a little nervous, for the corps was about to undergo the searching inspection of the General commanding the 19th corps d'armée, of which our regiment was a unit.

Only those who have assisted as an actor in an ordeal of this kind, can fully appreciate the nervous tension produced on all present by the last few minutes of waiting prior to the event.

The previous day, and indeed part of the night, has been spent in preparations.

"Troops to be paraded in full campaigning order"—so ran the general command; and in consequence there were stores and ammunition to be served out in addition to the ordinary work which devolves on the private and his superiors previous to a big review. Into the preceding twenty-four hours has been crammed as much hustling, rushing, brushing, scrubbing, polishing as the men and their officers can be expected to support; and now that the activity has been suddenly succeeded by a dead calm, and the query has arisen in the minds of all present as to whether everything necessary to the upholding of the good traditions of the corps has been done, the three thousand rank and file present and their chief can be reasonably excused the feeling of nervous tension which pervades them, and which owes its origin to the brusque reaction of the change from febrile activity to silent and immobile expectancy.

At such moments the most trivial incidents, which at ordinary times would pass unnoticed, will produce a general impression, even as a tiny twig falling into a well will create a ripple on the surface of its water.

Impressed, perhaps, by the silence of the motionless men around him, the Colonel's charger arches his beautiful neck, paws the stone pavement and whinnies. The mounts of the majors and company commanders take up and echo his shrill cry, break into little impatient movements, and are at once curbed by their riders. The incident, if so it can be called, is over in less time than it takes to describe; but even this banality has sufficed to provoke a grin which passes on from face to face, until a wave of still and nervous mirth ripples across the features of all.

Some one's steel-shod rifle-butt, breaking the tense silence, clangs on the stones, and one can almost feel the passing of the silent curses which, quicker than thought, go out from each to the comrade for his carelessness. Then in the distance there is a sound—at first a murmur—which as it approaches gains volume, until the noise of trotting hoofs and the occasional clink of steel can be distinguished.

All eyes are at once turned to the barrack railings and the gate with its flanking guard house. Beyond this, on the opposite pavement, can be seen the expectant crowd, composed of a big element of French and Spanish colonists in ordinary European attire, many stately Arabs clad in long white burnous, and head-dress of the same colour, which is secured with the usual cord of camel's hair; a sprinkling of Algerian Jews in baggy knickerbockers and gaudy-hued embroidered jackets, and here and there a few native women of the lower classes, most of whom wear the haik or long veil which conceals their hair and all their features save the eyes, unless they be of Kabyle blood, and expose their small and comely traits.

The faces of the crowd are all turned in one direction, their hands raised, shading their eyes from the glare of the African sun, which brings out, with almost painful vividness, the bright dashes of colour in their costumes, as they gaze eagerly towards the approaching cavalcade, the sound of which is now so near that it mingles with the sharp words of command, and the rattle of the rifles of the guard at the gate as they come to the salute. The Colonel draws his sword, and spurs his charger forward a few paces.

From the "adjudant major" comes the sharp order, "Garde à vous!" and there is a rustle along the ranks as the men stiffen up to attention.

Then, "Bayonnettes aux canons!" A sharp rattle, and the lines are tipped with steel.

Suddenly through the iron railings can be seen a rush of bright colours, and the General and his escort are in view. Coming along, almost at a gallop, he turns sharply and enters the gate; and as he does so, the Colonel, who then faces him, brings his sword up to the salute, and the command rings out "Portez armes!"—"Presentez-armes!" each order being followed by the short, crisp "crash!" of three thousand smartly-handled rifles.

From the men in the crowd outside come cries of "Vive la France!" "Vive la Légion!" And the native women join in the din with their repeated yells of "How! How! How!" The flag is unfurled, and floats out proudly on the light breeze.

There is a glare of polished brass, as forty bugles are brought up with a jerk to as many mouths, and they blare out the salute to the flag "Au Drapeau."

The General, who has drawn up his charger with a jerk, and sits with his right hand brought up to the peak of his white-plumed cocked hat, is in the full uniform of a commander of a corps d'armée, and his escort of Arab cavalry, in red cloaks and blue and white turbans, which has halted just inside the gates after wheeling smartly into line, forms a most picturesque background, which shuts out from sight the eager, shouting throngs in the street.

The General, and indeed all the officers and troops present, remain at the "Salut," until the last notes from the bugles die away; and then comes the order, "Portez armes," a rattle—and all is still again.

The detailed inspection of the troops and their quarters terminated, the regiment is marched out to the parade ground, where manœuvres are gone through, the duration of which depends entirely on the whim of the Inspector-General.

However, these rarely last more than two hours, and then the corps marches back to barracks through the town, much to the delight of the Arab population, who are a warlike people and thoroughly enjoy a military pageant.

Also the Legion presents a pleasing sight to a soldier's eyes, as with bayonets fixed the men swing by, each battalion, company and file at its proper distance. The tramp of feet resounds with clockwork regularity, in union with the musical rhythm of the band, and the blare of the bugles, crashing out the regimental march with its rattling chorus, the words seeming to hover over the lips of all the men:

"Tiens voila du boudin! voila du boudin! voila du boudin!
Pour les Alsaciens, les Suisses et les Lorrains,
Pour les Belges il n'y en a point,

Pour les Belges il n'y en a point,
Car ce sont des tireurs au flanc.
Pour les Belges il n'y en a point,
Pour les Belges il n'y en a point,
Car ce sont des tireurs au flanc."

No other regiment in France can approach the Legion for smartness at drill and on parade. The men are proud of the reputation, and make every effort to maintain it.

The bands of the 1st and 2nd Régiments Étrangers are of the best. That of the first of these corps is particularly good, and it possesses a weird and barbaric sort of musical instrument—if so it can be called—which was captured in an engagement with the troops of the famous Arab chief Abd-el-Kader, some sixty years ago.

It consists of a haft of polished hard wood about 5 feet long; at the top of this is a big silver crescent, and below, at intervals of about 6 inches one from the other, and on either side are five metal brackets, the ends of which are decorated with long streamers of horse-hair dyed a bright red. From these are suspended a multitude of small silver bells, producing a gay and exhilarating sound when shaken in cadence with the music. When the regiment is on the march the detachment of sappers is several paces ahead of the band.

Like their confrères in our own army these men carry axes, spades and saws; the original idea of their presence there being, I suppose, that they might clear the route for the troops behind.

However, taking into consideration the existing railways and good roads of to-day, one may safely conclude that their presence in modern infantry corps is due rather to a respect for tradition than to actual utility.

The corporal who was in command of the sappers, at the time I am writing of, was the biggest man in the regiment. He was six feet four, and broad in proportion. He was of Belgian nationality, and called Mertens, and was the hero of an episode of which all the regiment was justly proud. This incident took place at the capture of the fortified town of Sontay, in Tonquin, on the 16th December, 1883, which place was defended at the time by Prince Hoang-Ke-View, governor of the province, with about twenty thousand troops, composed principally of Chinese blackflag braves.

When the fire from the French gun-boats and field artillery had made a breach in the thick walls of the city, Admiral Courbet, who was in command of the expedition, launched a battalion of Arab light infantry (Tirailleurs Algériens) against the position.

Notwithstanding the fact that these men were seasoned troops and born fighters, they were beaten back with severe loss, which speaks much for the desperate resistance offered by the Chinese garrison, some of whom were daring enough to dart out through the gap in the walls and decapitate the dead and wounded left in the track of the retreating column. The bleeding heads, placed atop of bamboo poles, were planted on the crest of the ramparts amid the shrill, triumphant yells of the Celestials.

The Arabs, reformed and stiffened by two companies of French marines, rushed once more to the assault, but with no more success, and indeed with greater loss than the first time. Now the white-faced, gory necked heads of some of the French marines balanced side by side with the dusky bleeding features of their African comrades. The Chinese, howling drunk with success, and heedless of the fire from the French artillery, which was covering the retreat, stood on the wall to yell defiance and invective at their enemy. Indeed, so greatly was the garrison encouraged that a sortie was made which threatened to develop into a strong attack on the flanks of the expeditionary force.

The Admiral then played his last and trump card, and a battalion of the Legion, which till now had formed part of the reserve, rushed at the breach with the band playing and colours flying.

These troops advanced at the pas de charge, and were met by a terrible fire; many fell, but they were not to be denied.

In a few minutes the first ranks reached the edge of the ditch, and leaping down on to the slope of débris, formed by the stones and earth detached by the cannonade, they scrambled up to the breach, tore away the bamboo palisade, rushed, or were pushed, through it, and gained the crest.

The Legionaries suffered fearful loss; and it is to be feared that, excited by this and the cruel murder of their wounded comrades, they gave little mercy to those who opposed them.

Among the first to gain a footing in the place were a subaltern bearer of the colours, and big Mertens.

The first was immediately shot dead, whereupon the sapper seized the flag, and, rushing to the ramparts, stood on them in view of the whole army. Waving the bullet-torn, powder-stained tricolour above his head, he shouted: "Vive la Belgique! Vive la Légion!"

There was something grimly comical, but truly typical, in the conduct of this mercenary, who, forgetting the country for which he was fighting, and after just risking death a hundred times, coupled in his shout of triumph the name of his motherland and that of the corps to which he belonged.

Mertens received the médaille militaire for his bravery; and it is reported that Admiral Courbet, when complimenting him on the courage he had shown, said: "And you would have had the Legion of Honour had you cried, 'Vive la France!'"

This last, however, is probably a soldier's yarn.

With September came the manœuvres which were held in the south of the province of Oran, and along the Morocco frontier towards the Tuat and the Figuig oases.

My battalion went by train as far as Mecheria, where the column was concentrated.

From this point we proceeded afoot to Ain-Sefra, and thence south, along the caravan routes into the desert.

It was terribly hard work marching through the sand under the scorching African sun, laden as we were with all our kit.

South of Ain-Sefra there is little or no vegetation, save at an occasional oasis. The landscape consists of stretches of sand hillocks, with here and there patches of mimosa and Alfa grass, the monotony being broken only at rare intervals by the brown tents of an Arab encampment.

Fuel was so scarce that it was necessary to burn dry camel dung for cooking purposes. We had been out about ten days when I fell ill with typhoid fever, and was sent back to Sidi-bel-Abbes.

The convoy of sick, of which I was a unit, travelled part of the way by camel or mule cacolet, and the remainder by rail.

It was a terrible journey, and the sufferings I endured will never be erased from my memory. Indeed, even to-day it is a source of wonder to me that I pulled through it, for I was in a sorry state when carried eventually into the military hospital of our garrison town.

During the latter part of my stay in the hospital I learnt from fellow-patients that a violent epidemic of typhoid had swept through the corps; and I was terribly grieved when, on my return to the barracks, I was told that my friend Knox had been among the first to be carried off by the scourge. I remained for a long time under the sad impression which his loss had caused me. He was a true friend and a good soldier, and, had he lived, would have carved out a place for himself in the regiment.

On rejoining my corps I was examined by our battalion surgeon, Dr Aragon, a kind and really clever medical officer, who liked "mes legionnaires," as he called us, but who was unsparing to malingerers who shammed sickness to shirk work.

He declared that I could not possibly go back to my duties for several weeks, so, on his recommendation, I was sent off to Arzew, a small and charming little seaport town, situated on the coast about 100 miles west of Oran. This city was the "Arsenaria" of the Roman Empire.

It possesses a fine natural harbour, and the ancients used to put in there with their vessels to escape from the westerly gales so prevalent on this coast.

A chain of hills, varying from 1,000 to 2,000 feet high, encompass the town landwards, and on these, facing the sea, are several forts.

One of these works of defence served as a sanatorium for the weak and convalescent men of the Legion who had returned from Tonquin, or who, like myself, were recovering from diseases contracted in Algeria.

The fort was splendidly situated on the crest of one of the hills, 1,200 feet above the sea, which washed its base. A pine-wood extended from the beach right up to the edge of the moat, and from the other side of the hill one could look right down into the town and count the red-tiled roofs, or the people in the market-place.

I stayed here during three months and recovered all my old strength and vigour, thanks to the pure air and rest I enjoyed during that period. My time there passed swiftly and pleasantly, for we were at liberty to go for many long walks, and indulge in as much sea-bathing as we liked.

There was also a small theatre fitted up in one of the casemates. The sergeant who was in charge of this, a most enthusiastic amateur, decided, though I could never explain his reason for so doing, that I possessed a latent talent for the stage, and he pressed me into the troupe to perform minor parts. At first reluctant, I soon found that there was a great deal of amusement to be got out of the rehearsals and performances.

I did not shine in men's rôles which it was my lot to fill, but when I appeared as the Alsatian maid-of-all-work in "La consigne est de ronfler" my success was unmistakable.

I am close on six feet, and the skirt and bodice which, an hour before the performance began, were given me to wear, had probably been made for a lady about five feet four. When attired, my dress reached a little below my knees, the sleeves finished just above my elbows, and a blonde wig, surmounted by a big silk bow, added another good two inches to my height.

If I can judge by the screams of laughter and thunderous applause which greeted my appearance each time I "went on," and by the hilarity of my fellow-actors, who sometimes failed to preserve their gravity when I gave them the "cue," I ought to consider that I made a palpable "hit" in a feminine part.

When I had been two months at Arzew I felt so much better that I applied to the garrison doctor for permission to return to my corps, and, after a medical examination, was authorised to do so.

I arrived at my former quarters in Bel-Abbes on the 20th January, 1891. A fortnight after my return an official announcement was made that a detachment of five hundred men, reliefs for the companies in Tonquin, would shortly be sent East, and that those desiring to volunteer should send in their names.

The conditions required were—good conduct, nine months' previous service, and a satisfactory examination by the doctors. It is needless to state that I applied at once, and my jubilation was great when, a month later, I was informed by my sergeant-major that I had been accepted.

On the morning of 2nd March, attired in our colonial service kit, we marched out of barracks to the station, escorted by the remainder of the regiment in review order. The Colonel and his staff, the band, and the colours were formed up on the platform. Our chief addressed a few well-chosen words to the detachment, wishing us a safe return, stating that he was confident that we would do our best at all times and under all conditions to maintain the splendid reputation of the corps.

Then, as our train slid slowly out of the station, the band struck up "The Marseillaise," the troops presented arms, and the colours were lowered. Our Colonel and his staff stood at the salute as we rolled by, and our comrades sent off cheer after cheer, to which we replied to the best of our ability. It was destined that I should not return as a Legionary to the headquarters of the regiment, but the enthusiastic send-off given by the corps to our detachment will never fade from my memory.

We stayed in Oran five days awaiting the arrival of the trooper.

Here we met with the most cordial hospitality from the regiment of Zouaves which garrisoned the town and in whose barracks we were quartered, and the popularity of our corps was clearly demonstrated by the repeated gifts of tobacco, pipes, books and games of all kinds which were made to us by civilians, and were destined to solace the tediousness of the long journey we were about to take.

Oran is too well known to the English tourist of to-day for it to be necessary to describe at length this picturesque old city; which in its history and situation resembles Algiers. Both were formerly the strongholds of the Moorish pirates who swept the Mediterranean during several centuries.

The whitewashed, red-tiled houses rise terrace above terrace, in the form of a crescent from the sea, and a heavy fortress palace known as the "Kasba," formerly the residence of the Bey, dominates the city and seems to hold it in submission.

On the 8th March, accompanied by an armed picquet and the band of the Zouaves, we marched down to the quay and embarked on the Bien-Hoa, a government transport of about 5,000 tons register, which sailed the same day. Besides our own detachment there were about six hundred men, reliefs for the Infanterie de Marine and batteries in Tonquin, and one hundred and fifty battery mules.

Fortunately for the French soldier of to-day, the Republic no longer undertakes the transport of her troops over seas, and these operations are confided to private firms who own big steamers, specially fitted out for the trade.

The advantages of this system are considerable, both from the point of view of economy to the Government and of comfort to the passengers. On board the Bien-Hoa the troops were submitted to the same discipline as the crew. We were divided into messes and watches, and had to take a turn at scrubbing the decks in the morning, hauling in and slacking the lead ropes at sail drill, and aiding in the several other duties of the ship, which a landsman can safely do without imperilling life and limb. We grumbled a great deal, for that is a soldier's prerogative; and were grumbled at still more for our clumsiness; but the work kept us fit, and was an excellent cure for those disposed to sea-sickness.

Frequent parades and kit inspections were also held by our own officers, and these did away with the tendency to slackness and loss of discipline which are the consequent results of the tedium and inaction of a long voyage. The food was good and plentiful. Fresh meat, vegetables and bread were served out four days in each week; salt beef or pork, dried beans or lentils, and ship's biscuits formed the menu of two days' meals; and Friday being a fast-day—for at that time the French navy still retained many Catholic institutions—meat was replaced by sardines and cheese. There was an abundance of good coffee and pure water at the disposal of thirsty men, and each private drew a daily ration of a pint of red wine.

Defaulters, however, were deprived of this wine during the term of the disciplinary punishment they had incurred.

All the military passengers, from the sergeants downwards, slept in hammocks slung in the 'tween decks, and, judging by my own experience, it is certain that many of us found this mode of accommodation far from comfortable during the first week or so. However, we all seemed to become reconciled to it in the long run, although, even towards the end of the voyage, I would have preferred to sleep on the deck, and I know there were many more of the same mind; but this was strictly forbidden.

There is certainly, if one can depend on what the sailors say—and they ought to know—a way of obtaining as much rest in a hammock as in a bed if one only knows how; but I am convinced, from experience, that to gain that knowledge one must serve a long apprenticeship and begin it when young.

Some very good concerts were organised on board, and these, together with the exciting games of draughts, dominoes or loto, were of great help in assisting us to pass the time when we were not at drill, on duty, or undergoing inspection.

The aumônier or chaplain of the ship was a great favourite with all. This kindly cleric was a fine specimen of manhood, who stood over six feet. His erect mien and the grey beard which fell on his black soutane gave him a most apostolic and benevolent exterior, which was justified by the really good, gentle and merry soul it contained. He would often go out of his way to intercede with the commander in favour of a punished man, and have the guilty one sent to his cabin, where, by simple straight-spoken homilies, of which he knew the secret, he would appeal to the pride and manhood of his hearer.

More often than not he succeeded in moving the men to real emotion, and few were such fools as to be bold enough to interrogate the abashed and sometimes red-eyed delinquent who might be returning from a half-hour with the padre.

Neither did he confine his special attention to the souls of the few black sheep of his flock, for at the close of his admonitions he would often comfort the body of the repentant and affected sinner by administering a glass of Malaga taken from his own special bottle, which would be accompanied by more paternal advice concerning the future conduct of his cher garçon.

More than once did I remark this excellent man, when, after one of these interviews he would come from his cabin, and, leaning on the rail, gaze out at the expanse of blue water dancing in the tropical sunlight, and note on his benevolent features the gentle, contented smile which bespoke indulgence for the faults of others, and the satisfaction of a duty accomplished.

Our journey was a long one, for the ship, though a very seaworthy craft, could not steam more than twelve knots at her best. The engines broke down on two occasions, once in the Red Sea, when we were delayed for two days, and again in the Indian Ocean, where the trooper lay like a log for seventy hours before the necessary repairs could be effected.

For coaling purposes we touched at Colombo and Singapore, but remained only a few hours in these ports.

The Bien-Hoa arrived at Saigon on 13th April, and stayed there for four days, during which we were quartered in the barracks of the 11th Regiment of the Infanterie de Marine.

Here we were able to stretch our legs a little by going out and visiting the town, which is a fine one, and possesses a splendid Botanical Garden and zoological collection. Most of us were specially delighted at being able to sleep for a few nights in a cot again.

We sailed early in the morning of the 18th, and anchored in Along Bay (Tonquin) on the evening of the 21st April.

Here we saw for the first time the land we had all been so impatient to reach, and from which many of us were destined never to return, and speculations were rife concerning the military operations going on. We were all agreeably surprised to find, after our experience of the damp, depressing heat of Saigon, that the climate here was quite supportable, and resembled somewhat that of a warm spring day in Europe. However, we were soon to make acquaintance with the tropical summer of Tonquin, which usually sets in about the middle of May—that is to say, as soon as the south-west monsoon is well established, when the terrible intensity of its heat is all the more appreciable owing to the suddenness of its arrival.

CHAPTER III

France possesses an empire of no small importance in the East, the total area of which, some 256,000 square miles, is more than three times greater than her home territory. French Indo-China, which includes Cochin-China, Cambodia, the Laos country, Annam and Tonquin, consists, roughly speaking, of the basins of the two great rivers, the Mekong and the Song-Koï (Red River), and is situated between 8 deg. 30 min. and 23 deg. 23 min. N. lat., and 97 deg. 40 min. and 108 deg. 30 min. E. long. The total population is about 24,000,000.

Tonquin forms the north-eastern extremity of French Indo-China. It is bounded on the north by the Chinese provinces of Yunan and Kwang-si, on the west by the Laos provinces, on the south by Annam and the Gulf of Tonquin, and on the east by the Chinese province of Kwang-tung. Its total area is about 35,000 square miles, and it contains a population of over 12,000,000.

Near the sea the country consists of a rich alluvial plain intersected by numerous waterways, the principal one being the Red River, which rises in Yunan, and empties itself into the Gulf of Tonquin. From about 100 miles inland the ground rises gradually, and the whole country breaks up into a confusing jumble of hills and rocky pinnacles, which as one proceeds further north and east become mountain ranges, some of the peaks on the Tonquin-Yunan frontier attaining a height of about 9,700 feet. Along the Kwang-si frontier there are also altitudes of some importance. Attached to the great mountain chains of north and middle Tonquin, there are numerous series of lesser heights, which diminish as they come towards the south. The hills are covered with a dense grass higher than a man's shoulders; the mountains with thick, impenetrable forests. The rich alluvial plain or Delta, which extends from the sea, is densely populated, and produces yearly two very important rice crops.

The country was originally inhabited by a race known as the Kmers, who, if one can judge by the rare specimens of their architecture which exist along the coast of Annam, attained a comparatively high standard of civilisation.

At an epoch which it is impossible to designate with any exactitude, but which can be placed with some probability about 2,500 B.C., the Kmers were overwhelmed by an Annamese invasion, and almost exterminated.

The survivors fled northwards towards the mountains and high tablelands difficult of access, leaving the rich Delta plains in the hands of their conquerors. The numerous mountain tribes of to-day, known as the Muongs, Mans and Thos, which are to be found in the highlands of Annam and Tonquin, are most probably the descendants of the former owners of the country.

As a race they are superior both in physique and courage to the Annamese, although they do not possess the cunning and craftiness of this race.

It was probably owing to a want of cohesion and organisation, or to the fact that the invaders possessed better weapons and superior methods of warfare, that they were driven from their homes. In speech, appearance, dress and customs, these aborigines bear a striking resemblance to the mountain tribes who inhabit the interior of the islands of Hainan and Formosa, and it is probable that they belong to a once-powerful race which existed at a distant period along the littoral of Eastern Asia. Their skin is of a very light yellow tint; some of the women are almost white.

Their features are small and regular, and they do not possess the narrow eyes, flat noses, prominent cheek bones and enormous mouths of the Annamese. They are also taller, stronger, and present a much healthier appearance.

Their costume consists of a cotton blouse and short trousers reaching just below the knee, the uniform colour being a deep blue.

These people wear their hair very long, and it is wound round the top of the head and enclosed in a turban of similar colour and texture to their costume. Like some of the natives of the Laos provinces and the Yunan, the Muongs always wear a sort of puttie, made of blue cotton cloth, which is wound round the leg from ankle to knee.

They are expert mountaineers and hunters, and will not hesitate in attacking a tiger or panther with no better weapons than poisoned arrows, or a matchlock gun.

The origin of the Annamese or Tonquinese—for they are one and the same race—is very obscure, since they possess no reliable records going back for more than eight centuries, which is considerably posterior to the epoch at which their ancestors must have invaded Indo-China.

Some writers declare them to be of Mongolian origin, though this is hardly probable, for, if one can judge by the territory the race actually occupies, they probably came from the south-west. Others have declared them to be a branch of the Malay family.

In physique they resemble the Siamese, and are not so sturdy as the Malay. Their skin is of a deep copper colour. They are very small, their average height being about 4 feet 10 inches. Their lower members are strong and well formed, but the bust is long, thin and weak.

The everyday costume of the men consists of a kind of jacket and trousers of cotton cloth reaching almost to the ankles, the colour of which is generally a dark brown. The garments of the women are somewhat similar, but over those already mentioned they wear a sort of long stole which falls almost to the feet.

Both sexes wear their hair very long; it is rolled up in a strip of silk or cotton cloth, and wound round the head like a turban.

Their features are far from pleasing—indeed, one might qualify them as almost repulsive; flat noses with distended nostrils, high, receding foreheads, prominent cheek bones, narrow eyes and an enormous mouth being their principal traits.

Their character also presents few good points. That they are intelligent and possess a wonderful power of assimilation there can be no doubt, but these good traits are negatively qualified by the enormous amount of vanity, laziness, cruelty and cunning with which they are gifted.

Buddhism and ancestor-worship form the base of their religion, which is as strongly impregnated with Chinese ideas as is their language with words of the same origin, this being the natural result of their conquest by that race in the year 116 B.C., from which epoch to the arrival of the French the kingdom of Tonquin formed a fief of the Celestial Empire.

The influence of France in Indo-China dates back to 1585 when a Jesuit Father, Georges de la Mothe, established several missions, homes and schools at different points in the Mekong Delta.

Owing to the activity of the French Fathers the influence of that country increased enormously; and in November, 1787, thanks to Bishop Pigneau de Béhaine, who was at that time the trusted friend and counsellor of the Emperor Gia-Long at Hué, a treaty was signed at Versailles by Louis XVI. and Cang-Dzue, son of the above-mentioned sovereign. By this treaty the French king placed at the disposal of his Eastern ally a naval squadron composed of twenty men-of-war, five European regiments and two native ones; also a sum of 1,000,000 dollars, of which 500,000 were in specie, and the remainder in arms and munitions of war. In return for these favours the Emperor of Annam made territorial concessions in the Island of Poula Condor and at Tourane to the French nation.

On his death in 1820 Gia-Long was succeeded by his son Tu-Duc, who detested the Europeans. The French settlers were driven from their concessions, and the missionaries persecuted and massacred.

Being at this epoch engrossed by the political situation in Europe, it was not until the end of 1858 that the French Government was able to undertake active measures for the protection of her interests.

In that year the port of Tourane was captured, and in February, 1859, Saigon, the capital of Cochin-China, was also taken.

From the occupation of these two ports may be said to begin the era of French conquest in Indo-China, of which the principal events are the following:

1867. Capture of Finh-Larg, Sa-dec, Cho-doc and Hatien (Cochin-China).

1873. Capture of Hanoï (capital of Tonquin) by Francis Garnier.

1879. Cochin-China declared a French colony, with Saigon as the capital.

1883. Insurrection of the Black Flags in Tonquin, which was secretly encouraged by the Emperor Tu-Duc. Massacre of Francis Garnier and Commandant Rivière near Hanoï. Death of Tu-Duc. Treaty signed at Hué by the Regent Hiep-Hoa, acknowledging the French Protectorate over Annam and Tonquin.

1884. Defeat of the Black Flags by Admiral Courbet at Nam-Dinh, Bac-Ninh and Son-Tay. Rupture with China, who refused to renounce her feudal rights.

1885. Signature of the treaty with China, by which that country renounces all sovereignty over Tonquin. Rebellion at Hué suppressed by the General de Courcy. Capture of the young Emperor Ham-Nghi, who was exiled to Algeria, the French Government placing his half-brother Than-Thai on the throne.

In 1886 M. Paul Bert was appointed first Governor of Indo-China. The kingdom of Annam and the Tonquin Delta were placed under the administration of Residents with a Civil staff.

From this it must not be imagined that the pacification of the country was complete. The treaty of 1885, which secured the evacuation by the Chinese army of the provinces of Lao-Kay, Ha-Giang, Cao-Bang and Lang son, had put a stop to any organised warfare; and the exile of the young Emperor Ham-Nghi to Algeria in the same year had crushed the open resistance of the court of Hué. However, thousands of Black Flag soldiers and Hunan braves had remained in Tonquin, and these occupied the mountainous regions in the north and east of that country, from which they descended at intervals to prey on the rich villages and towns in the plains, and to harass or capture the outlying French garrisons.

In Hué also there were many mandarins, who, though they openly professed friendship to France and acknowledged the sovereignty of Than-Thai, were partisans of the exiled monarch, and secretly subventioned and organised insurrections in the provinces of Than Hoa (Annam), Son-Tay, Bac-Ninh, Thaï-Nguyen and the Yen-Thé (Tonquin).

These officials were also in communication with the Chinese bands, three of whose principal leaders, Ba-Ky, Luong-Tam-Ky and Luu-Ky, were former lieutenants of the old Black Flag General, Lieu-Vinh-Phuoc.

In 1891, when I arrived in Tonquin, the political situation of the colony was little better than in 1885, so far as the question of general pacification was concerned. The Delta provinces had accepted the French rule, and the principal towns were growing in importance and prosperity under a wise system of administration, but the neighbouring provinces were rampant with brigandage and open revolt. Organised resistance to the new order of things existed within a few miles of Hanoï the capital, and Haïphong the seaport, of the colony.

Indeed, as late as in 1892 the suburbs of the first-mentioned were on several occasions attacked, looted and partially burnt; and in 1891 the Chinese bands who occupied the mountainous region known as the Bao-Day would raid the villages on the left bank of the Cua-Cam, and out of sheer bravado fire a volley or two over the river into Haïphong.

Military columns were sent out each winter, but with small results. Before these forces the bands would retire to their rocky highland fortresses, and to reach them the troops had to pass through many miles of most difficult country, covered with dense forest and jungle, and traversed by few paths, the whereabouts of which were kept secret by the enemy.

Information was most difficult to obtain, the fear of the Chinese being so great that even their victims refused to give the officers any aid in the matter, knowing full well that reprisals would follow.

Frequently disasters would occur, and a reconnoitring party would be cut up in a narrow defile, or a convoy ambuscaded and captured. From 1887 to 1891 each successive General commanding the troops in the colony had urged on the Government the necessity of undertaking operations on a more extensive scale than heretofore; and had these officers been allowed a free hand in the matter, there is little doubt that this chronic state of insurrection and anarchy would have been brought to a speedy end.

But the Ministry in Paris would not hear of such a thing. In France the mere mention of the word "Tonquin" raised a babble of excited recriminations. The public would have none of it.

In 1883, 1884 and 1885 nearly fifteen thousand of the flower of the French army had perished of disease, or had been slain by a merciless enemy.

The expedition had cost hundreds of millions of francs, and the large army of soldiers it was still necessary to maintain in the colony was of great expense each year to the metropolis. The majority of Frenchmen who had never at any time possessed serious cravings for a Colonial Empire, were tired of the whole business.

Right up to 1890 it was seriously debated in the Chamber, on different occasions, whether it would not be better to abandon this new colony. Fortunately for France she retained her rich prize.

The Tonquin question had caused a hetacomb of Ministries.

Jules Ferry, France's greatest politician since Gambetta, owed his downfall to Général de Négriers reverse at Ky-Lua, and the subsequent retreat of the army from Lang-son. Notwithstanding his undoubted talents he was never able to recover his former influence in State affairs.

In 1885 the excited Parisian mob would have torn him to pieces had he fallen into their hands.

"À bas Ferry!" "À bas le Tonkinois!" was their cry.

To-day every serious Frenchman acknowledges his respect for this great statesman, who was undoubtedly the founder of the splendid Colonial Empire his country possesses.

From 1887 to 1891, owing to the state of public opinion, it became absolutely necessary for succeeding Ministers, who had any respect for the stability of their portfolios, to adopt a special line of conduct in regard to Tonquin, which might be defined as a policy of mild procrastination.

Instructions were given to the Governors of the unhappy colony which might be summed up as, "Don't ask for more men; don't ask for more money. Do the best you can with what you have, and make no noise over it."

In consequence, the Governors were obliged to repress the legitimate aspirations of the military officers, and refused to sanction operations on an extensive scale, which, though necessary, would most probably attract public attention in France. The natural result of this situation was that during the whole of this period the relations between the civil and military powers in the colony were of the worst. In the French Chamber the Ministry would announce from time to time that the work of pacification was making rapid strides, that organised resistance was at an end, and that the occasional depredations which occurred—the importance of which, they stated, was magnified by the sensational press of the metropolis—were the acts of a few stray Chinese brigands (Voleurs de Vaches), whom the local militia and gendarmes were quite able to bring to order. In the meanwhile, the bands aforementioned, secure in the comparative inactivity of the French, continued to plunder the villages and capture the native authorities, who were liberated after payment of a ransom. In 1889 the famous Luu-Ky succeeded in carrying off three French colonists, the two brothers Rocque and Baptiste Costa. They were surprised whilst on a shooting expedition a few miles from Haïphong. They remained prisoners of the band for upwards of two months, and suffered every possible indignity and great privations. They were finally liberated on the payment of 80,000 dollars.

Encouraged by the success of their compatriots, the Chinese soldiers, who garrisoned the blockhouses and forts along the Kwang-si and Kwang-tung frontiers, would leave their uniforms behind them and pass into the provinces of Lang-son and Cao-Bang, where they would raid the rich valleys, burn the villages, drive away the cattle, slaughter the male inhabitants, and carry back the women into captivity.

In the Yen-Thé the partisans of Ham-Nghi, who were secretly encouraged by the mandarins in Hué, had raised the standard of revolt.

They occupied strong and well-fortified positions, possessed an abundance of arms and ammunition, and were ably generalled by De-Nam, a former military mandarin of the exiled Emperor, who received tribute in money or rice from the majority of the rich villages in the Upper Delta, the inhabitants of which undoubtedly sympathised with the rebels, and aided them by every means in their power.

Such was the position of affairs in the Tonquin in April, 1891.

On the morning of the 22nd April our detachment was taken on board one of the small but well-built river steamers which resemble in form the boats running on the Mississippi.

These vessels are of very light draught, owing to the numerous shallows which exist in the upper reaches of the Tonquin rivers. After dodging around for more than an hour among the innumerable high stalactite rocks, covered with dwarfed vegetation, which tend to make Along Bay one of the most curious and picturesque spots in the world, our steamer entered one of the numerous estuaries by which the Song-Thuong and Song-Cau rivers empty themselves into the sea. The banks on either side were of soft mud, covered as far as the eye could reach with mangroves.

The water, which in the bay had been of a green tint, was now of a dark red-brown, and presented a consistency of good pea-soup.

Far away to the north-east could be discerned the high spurs of the mountain range increasing in altitude, and extending towards the Kwang-si and Kwang-tung frontiers. But the sight of these was soon lost, as from one estuary we passed into another, and the landscape became one monotonous stretch of mangrove swamp over which the damp atmosphere seemed to dance in the bright sunlight. At last, after rounding a sudden curve, we caught our first glimpse of Haïphong, which, owing probably to the continued and depressing vista we had just been subjected to, had the appearance of quite a big town.

At the time of which I am writing this city had emerged from its chrysalis state of a town built of mud upon mud, and a considerable transformation was taking place.

Whatever may have been the errors made by France with regard to the economical and political administration of her colonies in the past, she was, and still is, undoubtedly our superior as a builder of towns; and the case in point may well serve as a demonstration of the fact.

In 1884, Haïphong, a Sino-Tonquinese seaport, was an agglomeration of miserable dwellings constructed for the most part of mud, bamboo and matting, inhabited by natives, with here and there a few decent brick buildings occupied by a small number of Europeans and Chinese merchants.

It was situated in a swamp, and certain quarters of the town were invaded by the high tides several times each month. During the summer the blazing tropical sun converted the place into a cesspool. It reeked with disease, and cholera and malaria were ever rampant.

Seven years later, when I first saw the city, it presented the appearance of a well-built European centre; possessed floating wharves, well-laid-out streets, fine boulevards and good roads. An excellent system of surface drainage was being laid down, and the thoroughfares and many of the buildings were already lighted by electricity.

Since 1891 Haïphong has steadily increased in area and importance, and is now an up-to-date, progressive city.

Our steamer only stayed here about an hour, the time required to draw a day's rations for the detachment.

We now learnt that our destination was Phulang-Thuong, an important town situated on the Song-Thuong, about 65 miles inland from Haïphong, at which place the depot of the 2nd Battalion of our regiment was stationed.

We were soon off again, and to our relief the aspect of the surrounding country became a more hospitable one.

The flat expanse of slime, mud and mangroves had disappeared. Now the river ran in between high artificial embankments; beyond these, on either side, could be seen a well-cultivated plain whose only limit was the horizon, and which was divided up by low banks of earth into holdings of every shape and size. It had the appearance of an enormous fantastic chessboard, on which none of the divisions were of the same dimensions and few of them rectangular. All of them, however, were of the same colour—green; not green of a uniform shade, for each field seemed to possess a different nuance of that colour, from the light, nearly yellow, tint of the freshly-planted rice, to the dark, almost brown, hue of the tobacco plant.

If the first impression one receives from the Delta landscape be a pleasing one, this is due to the novelty of the scenery, and soon wears off. Its place is taken by a sense of weariness, owing to the ever-recurring sameness of the vista; and the eyes are fatigued by the crude, garish brilliancy of the verdure, the uniform blue of an almost cloudless sky, and the painful reflection of the bright tropical sunshine on the water in the paddy fields.

The uniformity of the plains of the Delta provinces is broken by the numerous hamlets surrounded by a ditch and an embankment, on the crest of which is a dense, impenetrable thicket or hedge of live bamboo, reaching up as high as 20 or 30 feet. In the interior of these villages each hut possesses a garden or plantation which is a tangled mass of luxuriant tropical vegetation, and through this from outside one can catch but faint glimpses of the brown thatched roofs of the dwellings. Plantains, guava, persimmon and custard-apple trees abound here.

Coming straight out of this wealth of foliage are clumps of tall, stately areca palms, which, as they tower above the homesteads, seem to gaze out into the plain like sentries, whose duties it might be to warn the villagers of the approach of the yak (pirates).

Close by the majority of these hamlets, situated generally on a slight eminence, and in the shade of one or more ancient banyan trees, are fine pagodas with quaintly-sloping, red-tiled roofs, and curved eaves, the crests of these being ornamented with gruesome-looking dragons and griffins. When the village is rich the temple is surrounded by a whitewashed wall, the upper portion of which is a kind of open trellis-work in brick, with a doorway flanked by tall, curiously-shaped columns, each surmounted by a many-hued, hideous plaster genie.

It was easy to see that the population was very dense in this part of the Delta. Hard at work in the fields were many natives, the majority of whom were women. There were others winding their way along the narrow paths which top the small banks separating each holding, or on the rough roads upon the summit of the embankments which accompany the sinuosities of the river.

These were in batches of from ten to thirty individuals, each carrying upon his or her shoulder a light bamboo, 4 feet long. Suspended from both extremities was a basket containing rice, vegetables, or some other local product which they were conveying to the nearest market for sale. These natives moved at a sort of jog-trot which gives a spring to the bamboo pole they carry, thus relieving them in a measure of the weight suspended at either end.

They can carry as much as 70 pounds during eight hours each day (that is exclusive of occasional rests), and they go at an average pace of 3 miles an hour.

The Tonquinese of both sexes wear enormous hats made from the leaves of the macaw palm. Those worn by the men are pointed at the top, and bear a strong resemblance in shape to a big paper lamp-shade. The weaker sex possess a headgear circular in form and flat on the top, around the edge of which is an inverted brim which shields the face and neck of the wearer from the horizontal rays of the sun. These hats have often a diameter of as much as 30 inches.

Four hours after we left Haïphong the aspect of the country underwent a decided change, and low hills were frequent. They increased in number and height as we went on, and the river soon wound its way between the first spurs of the Bao-Day range. This is a group of hills known as the "Ninety-nine Summits," which vary considerably in height from an altitude of 600 to 1,800 feet. All of them are covered with long grass, affording an excellent pasture for the cattle belonging to the numerous villages established in the valleys.

Although it was almost dusk the view from our little steamer was a varied and pleasing one, as the river twisted and turned between these almost cone-shaped elevations. Sometimes it seemed as if a big hill had slipped right into the river and blocked the way; but the stream would narrow and go right round its base, and, as we swept by, we could look straight up the side of the slope. At such times we could not refrain from thinking of what might happen if a few enterprising rebels took up a position on the side of such a hill. They could have fired volleys on to our crowded decks, and from such an angle that we could not have replied with the machine gun fixed on the roof forward.

However, fortunately for us, nothing of the kind did happen.

We arrived at Phulang-Thuong at nine o'clock in the evening, and having disembarked were quartered in an enormous pagoda which could easily have accommodated another five hundred men.

Each soldier was provided with a straw mattress and a blanket, and it was not long before silence and sleep reigned supreme. The picquet and guard were supplied from the garrison, for we were as yet unarmed. During the next day rifles, ammunition, and a khaki campaigning kit were served out to us. At this time putties were not worn in the French army; they have, however, been adopted since the 1900-01 campaign in China.

Each man made his own cloth leggings or gaiters, which reached about half-way up the calf of the leg, and were buttoned at the side. I should here remark that the French infantryman, whilst in the Colonies, wears a white sun-helmet, similar in shape to the one served out to our own troops, and, like the latter, it has a removable cover of khaki cloth.

The rifles we received were of the "-74 Gras Model." These, however, were replaced by "-86 Lebel Model" in May of the following year. The latter is a small calibre, smokeless powder, repeating weapon.

I was included in a batch of sixty men who were to reinforce the 1st Company of the 2nd Battalion, quartered at Nha-Nam, about 21 miles to the north of Phulang-Thuong.

There is a good road between these two points, which is constructed on an embankment 4 feet above the level of the surrounding paddy fields. It has probably been in existence for several centuries, and it is certainly one of the old mandarin routes, which were made throughout lower Tonquin by order of the Emperor Le-Vrang-Tong, who reigned during the latter part of the sixteenth century.

On the morning of the 24th April our detachment crossed the Song-Thuong river by the ferry, and stepped out briskly towards our new garrison.

We were under the orders of a sergeant-major, who, owing probably to the instructions he had received, organised the little column in a strictly regulation manner: with vanguard, rear-guard and flankers. These precautions led to speculations among us as to whether we should get through our first day of service in the colony without smelling powder. The majority would certainly have hailed with delight any chance of a scrimmage, but we were destined to be disappointed in that respect—for the time being, at all events. We reached Cao-Thuong about midday, at which place we partook of a meal cooked by ourselves. On the 6th November, 1890, an important engagement had taken place here between the rebels—who occupied a strongly-fortified position—and a French column of about twelve hundred men. This combat, which may be considered the first blow struck at the partisans of the exiled Emperor Ham-Nghi, was the opening engagement in a lengthy struggle lasting nearly three years, and which transformed large, well-cultivated, densely-populated plains into desolate tracts of country, overgrown with jungle, dotted here and there with the charred and blackened ruins of once flourishing villages.

That part of Tonquin known as the Yen-Thé region is bordered on the south and west by the Song-Cau river, on the east by the Song-Thuong, and on the north by a chain of rocky heights running from Thaï-Nguyen to Vanh-Linh, which is situated a little to the north of the new railway from Phulang-Thuong to Lang-son. The southern part of it, which is generally designated as the Lower Yen-Thé, is an immense plain rising gradually to the north, and studded here and there with small isolated groups of hills, none of which exceed 500 feet in height. It is traversed by numerous streams all running into the Song-Thuong and Song-Cau rivers, and to these the district owes its wonderful fertility.

The soil of this region is composed of a dull-red clay, containing innumerable small round pebbles. It does not produce such fine rice as the black alluvial mud plains of the Delta, but it is better adapted than these for the growing of yams, tobacco, the mulberry tree and castor-oil plant.

About 20 miles north of Phulang-Thuong this plain terminates, and it is succeeded by a mass of hills which here and there enclose small marshy plains. The country is overrun by dense forests, into which a few paths, made by charcoal burners, offer the only means of penetration.

It would need a master-pen to produce an adequate description of the savage wildness of this region, which teems with game. Tigers, panthers, bears, many kinds of deer, wild pigs and boars abound; peacocks, silver-pheasants, partridges and snipe are very numerous.

For centuries past the Tonquinese have associated the Upper Yen-Thé with the mysterious and the supernatural. Native folk-lore declares that a former Emperor, thanks to a powerful magic he possessed, succeeded in driving from the lowlands a race of cruel and wicked genii. To escape complete destruction these fled into the forests, where, so runs the legend, they still live and guard the rich mineral treasures which are said to exist there.

The native of the Delta possesses a real dread of this part of the country, for, not only is the Tonquinese the most superstitious of humans, but the lowlander who comes into these regions is speedily attacked by a virulent form of paludo-hæmaturic fever, which in most cases terminates fatally.

It was owing principally to these reasons that the native troops, with the exception of the few companies recruited from the Muong tribes, were of small service during the operations which took place there.

In this maze of hills, covered by virgin forests, rank swamp and deep jungle, De-Nam established his headquarters in 1887. He was no commonplace individual, this Asiatic; indeed, when one considers his subsequent career, it is impossible to repress a sentiment of admiration for this man, who, during the four years he led the rebellion, proved himself to be a capable administrator, a talented military engineer, and a clever and a daring general.

He belonged to the literati, or educated class, and was born near Dap-Cau, a town on the Song-Cau river, in 1836. Like his father, he became a mandarin, and filled successively several important posts in the Civil Administration of his country. On the establishment of the French Protectorate he withdrew to Hué, the capital of Annam; but on the exile of Ham-Nghi he returned to his birth-place, and began secretly to organise the insurrection in the province of which he was a native, aided, as it has already been stated, by covert encouragement and subsidies from some of the high native officials at the Court.

His choice of the Yen-Thé as a centre of resistance to the French was in itself no small proof of the acumen the man possessed. Apart from the difficulties which the surface configuration of the region offered to the movements of European troops, the natives were stronger and more courageous than those of the Delta, and it was from them that the greater part of the old army of Tu-Duc was recruited. After the capture of the citadels of Son-Tay and Bac-Ninh by the French, these troops, abandoned by their Black Flag allies, returned to their homes, concealed their arms, and, with the suppleness innate in the Asiatic, became for the time being peaceful cultivators of their native soil.

Their minds were, however, deeply imbued with the delights of their past career—the satisfaction based on a sense of swaggering superiority over their unarmed compatriots, and the consequent facilities which had existed for plundering them. The long "siestas," slack discipline, and numerous pipes of opium were still causes for keen regret, and they hated the monotony and hard work attached to the pursuit of agriculture. It is, therefore, easy to imagine with what eager joy these former warriors received the whispered appeal of secret propaganda—an appeal combining the glamour of patriotism with the promise of rapine, plunder, and the other joys so dear to the majority of Orientals—and the mysterious manner in which the message was communicated to them was in itself a fascination owing to their belief in the supernatural.

In 1888 the majority of the population of the Yen-Thé were fervent partisans of De-Nam, and but few villages had refused to throw in their lot with the insurgents. All the hamlets that abstained from joining the revolt were Catholic centres, for numerous missions of the Roman Church had been established in this district for more than a century.

It was at this time that the leader of the insurrection decided on building a fortified stronghold towards the north-east of Nha-Nam. A strong fort, rectangular in shape, with flanking bastions at each corner, was constructed. Within it were placed substantial native buildings capable of accommodating from six to eight hundred men. The position chosen was in a dense forest of which just the necessary area to be covered by the defensive work was cleared. Two narrow paths only led to it, and these approaches could be raked by cross-fires from the walls and bastions. The surrounding vegetation was so thick that it was impossible to make headway outside of the two tracks; and owing to its density, and to the fact that the position was situated in a slight hollow, there were no means of obtaining a glimpse of the fortifications until the first palisade, which enclosed them at a distance of about 25 feet, was reached. There were three of these palisades, and in the grass-covered space between them were planted numerous pointed bamboo stakes, the whole forming a most serious agglomeration of auxiliary defences.

The preceding details may apply to the numerous other defensive works subsequently erected by the rebels, all being on the same plan, and occupying similar sites.

From Hou-Thué—for this was the name given by the natives to the citadel—De-Nam administered the whole of the province in the name of the exiled Emperor. The villages paid taxes into his treasury, and furnished rice and other requisites for his army, which at this time consisted of about two thousand five hundred men, one thousand five hundred of whom were armed with breech-loading rifles.

The unfortunate hamlets which refused their support were mercilessly pillaged and burnt, and their inhabitants massacred as an example to other recalcitrants. It must, however, be stated, in justice to the rebel chief, that he protected those who were faithful to his rule, for, on several occasions, in 1889-90, he defeated detachments of native militia sent by the Resident in Bac-Ninh to collect taxes from the peasants. During this period the attention of the French authorities was so actively engrossed by the movements of the Chinese bands in the provinces of Lang-son and Cao-Bang on the Song-Koï and Black rivers, that action in the Yen-Thé was put off until the end of 1890.

As a natural result of this policy of tergiversation, the power and prestige of De-Nam increased considerably; and so great was his confidence in the ultimate success of the insurrection, that he established a strongly-fortified position at Cao-Thuong, in which he placed a garrison under the orders of De-Tam, the most trusted and capable of his lieutenants.

This subordinate not only administered the surrounding country, and levied toll in the name of his chief, but by night he often crossed the Song-Thuong and raided the rich villages around Phulang-Thuong, the inhabitants of which had been living in security and growing rich, thanks to the close proximity of the French troops garrisoned in that town. It was frequently the lot of the unhappy Resident to watch, through the night, from his verandah, the burning houses of these unfortunates.

Patrols would be sent out, but their departure was at once signalled, and they would arrive on the scene only to find that the raiders had decamped with their spoil; and sometimes these detachments, being at a disadvantage in the gathering darkness, would be ambuscaded by the rear-guard of the enemy, and suffer severe losses.

At last, something had to be done, and a column under General Godin was sent against the rebel position at Cao-Thuong. It was with some difficulty that the fort was located, owing to it being concealed in the midst of a dense thicket. Part of the expedition was surprised, and suffered losses. Eventually, thanks to the fire of half a battery of mountain guns, the position was evacuated, and the enemy, after breaking up into small groups, succeeded in escaping northwards. No dead or wounded Tonquinese were found in the fort, but its solid construction and the judicious selection of its site was cause for great surprise to all the officers present. There can be no doubt that in this, and also during the subsequent operations against Hou Thué, the French considerably underrated the strength and military capabilities of the enemy. It would not, however, be wise for us to criticise too severely, since we have committed similar errors in most of our own colonial expeditions.

A fine village close to the enemy's fort, was found to be abandoned, and was burned. With this the operations terminated, which fact demonstrates the ignorance of the French officials concerning the extent of the rising, for they now concluded, somewhat hastily, that the centre of resistance had been destroyed.

In reality the garrison of a small outpost only had been dislodged, and the enemy returned to the position as soon as the troops had gone. They did not, however, remain there long, for shortly afterwards the authorities constructed a strong fortification on the crest of a hill which overlooked all the surrounding country, and this was occupied by a detachment of native militia, under the orders of a French officer.

Elated with the knowledge that they had slain several French and native soldiers, the rebels most probably concluded that the victory had been theirs. Certain it is that for long afterwards every minstrel in the province sang of the prowess exhibited by De-Tam's troops on that day.

Before General Godin's column was broken up, the civil authorities decided on one wise measure. To ensure the tranquillity of the region after the taking of Cao-Thuong, a position was chosen at Nha-Nam, about 8 miles further north, and a fort was built there. A company of the Foreign Legion, one of native infantry with a mountain gun, and a few artillerymen were left behind to construct the fort.

Encouraged, no doubt, by the non-discovery of their strong positions in the north, and by the trifling loss they had sustained, the rebels became more venturesome than ever. Placards declaring war on the French Government, and threatening with death all natives who remained loyal to the foreigners, were posted up in the roads, by-ways and market-places of the province. Rich villages, situated but a mile or so from the garrison towns of Dap-Cau, Bac-Ninh and Phulang-Thuong, were pillaged, burnt, and many of the inhabitants slaughtered. Almost each night would see the troops under arms, and the sky reddened with a conflagration.

The civil authorities were supposed to supply intelligence to the military, and they had secret service funds at their disposal to pay for the work, but there was never any forthcoming. The enemy, however, were better served, and not an ambuscade could be planned or a patrol sent out but they were immediately informed of the fact. Towards the end of November a perfect state of anarchy, a veritable reign of terror, existed throughout the province; and, as a last resource, the Yen-Thé was placed under martial law, and the administration of the district entrusted to the Brigadier-General in command of the 2nd Brigade at Bac-Ninh.

To such as are cognisant with the French methods of recruiting the personnel of that country's colonial civil service, there is little cause for surprise at the maladministration of Tonquin at this period of its history. To have a parent in the Ministry, a relation who was a deputy, or an electioneering agent, or to possess a friend with political influence—these were the surest means of obtaining a soft, well-paid billet under the tropics. Few, if any, of the candidates nominated knew anything about the country, its people, their customs or language prior to their arrival in it; and even to-day, when some apology for a competitive examination has become necessary—though this is not always the case—not one in fifty of France's public servants in Indo-China possesses a sound knowledge of the vernacular.

Very shortly after matters had been taken in hand by the military authorities things began to take a turn for the better, thanks to sterner measures and a better organised system of espionnage.

When information had been obtained disclosing the existence of a strong main position at Hou-Thué, a reconnaissance was sent out from Nha-Nam on the 9th December to locate the route. This action led to a vague knowledge of the whereabouts of the enemy being obtained, and a small column, under Major Fane, marched against the rebels on the 11th.

After a good deal of skirmishing and groping about in the dense forest, the detachment, which had blundered blindly on the fortifications, was very severely handled and forced to retreat.

A new expedition, a thousand strong, under the command of Lieut.-Colonel Winckel-Meyer, attacked the rebels on the 22nd December. An attempt was made to assault the stronghold.

Owing to the fact that the enemy's works were only visible at a distance of a few yards, and also to the impracticability of clearing a road for the guns through the trees and undergrowth, it was found impossible to aid the attack by a preparatory action by the artillery. For a similar reason the assaulting party were obliged to move in Indian file along two narrow paths, exposed all the time to a severe cross-fire. Under such conditions the impetus so necessary to success was impossible, progress was slow, and casualties numerous.

The foliage was so dense that the few rays of the sun which pierced through it produced an effect of dim twilight. Through this semi-obscurity, which was intensified by the clouds of powder smoke which clung to the damp vegetation, could be distinguished the countless red flashes from the enemy's rifles. The continuous rattle of the musketry, the crashing clatter of the branches and twigs severed by the hail of lead, the insulting yells of the rebels, the monotonous boom of their war-drum, the complaints of the wounded and dying, produced a sensation of fearsome nightmare.

The European troops behaved splendidly. Those who escaped the zone of fire on the paths tried their best to break through the first bamboo fence, but were shot down almost as soon as they reached it. At one point a hole was made in the enclosure, and two Legionaries got through. They made a rush for the second palisade, but before they could reach it one of them fell, and his thigh was pierced by a pointed stake. Fortunately, his comrade succeeded in carrying him back the way they had come, and escaped himself without a scratch.

Unable to stand the continued strain, a company of native troops—tirailleurs Tonkinois—retreated in disorder. Some of them actually threw away their arms, and, with turbans gone, their long hair falling in confusion over their face and shoulders, fled shrieking and panic-stricken.

Seeing that success was not possible under the circumstances, the commander of the expedition wisely ordered a retreat. The engagement had lasted barely an hour, and over a hundred of the rank and file had been killed or wounded.

When the troops retired a good many of the slain, together with their arms and ammunition, fell into the hands of the rebels.

The column withdrew to Nha-Nam, and reinforcements of men, guns and mortars were sent from Bac-Ninh. Colonel Frey, who commanded the brigade, arrived, and took over the direction of the operations, which lasted from the 30th December to the 11th January, 1891.

Trenches were opened, but progress was very slow. Eventually, a position was reached about 100 yards from the first palisade, from which a glimpse of the interior of the fort could be obtained. A battery composed of two mountain guns and as many small mortars was established, and the shells thrown from them soon caused serious loss to the enemy, and set fire to one of the thatched roofs of the numerous buildings it contained. Most of these constructions were built of bamboo and plaster, so that the conflagration spread rapidly; and towards evening the interior of the citadel was a mass of flames. The rebels displayed striking courage, for they clung to the walls, and fired incessant volleys at the guns until late into the night. Profiting by the darkness, they then evacuated the fort, after burying their dead, and retired with their wounded to positions a few miles further north.

These positions were stronger than at Hou-Thué, and consisted of a big entrenched village, the approaches being covered by several forts and numerous rifle-pits, the importance of which was unknown to the French, so well had the secret of their construction been guarded.

On the following morning an assaulting column found the position at Hou-Thué empty, and the defences were partially destroyed by dynamite. After a few reconnoitring parties had been sent out, and no trace of the enemy discovered, the civil authorities concluded that the rebellion had been squashed, and the Governor gave orders for the column to be broken up.

However, to ensure tranquillity, it was decided to maintain the garrison, and strengthen the position at Nha-Nam, situate about 3 miles south-west of Hou-Thué, on a small elevation dominating to the south, east, and west the plain which extends towards the Song-Cau and Song-Thuong rivers, and northwards of which is the mass of forest-covered hills already described.

The garrison consisted of a company of the Legion, one of native infantry, and a mountain gun. The construction of the position went on very slowly, for the military authorities were able to obtain but few coolies, and the greater part of the labour had to be performed by troops who were continually harassed by night attacks; for the rebels, encouraged, no doubt, by the failure of the French to discover their new stronghold, were soon as active as before. Fortunately, the garrison experienced small loss, for the enemy contented themselves by firing into the place at night from a distance of about 300 yards.

The strain on the men was very great, however, as three or four nights a week they were under arms in expectation of an attempt to rush the position. This was the state of affairs when our detachment arrived at Nha-Nam on the evening of the 24th April.

Our arrival at the fort caused some little excitement, and numerous were the questions asked us concerning friends in Algeria.

We were at once distributed over the company, and I found myself placed in the second squad of the first section, which was lodged in a small pagoda, situated about 10 yards inside the fort gate, and almost facing it. This building was in very good condition, and faced the south. A vacant bed was given me, the former occupant of which, having been rather severely wounded in a skirmish about a fortnight previously, was in the hospital at Phulang-Thuong. I say bed, but in reality it was an apology for the comfortable cots used in Algeria. The trestles were of wood, and placed upon these was a plank about 2 feet broad. A regulation blanket folded in two served as a mattress. A good meal was awaiting us, and, after partaking of it, I arranged my kit, and in a quiet spot, with the help of a comrade, "washed down" with a bucketful of water.

Our long tramp, and the heat, had made us comfortably tired, so we turned in early and were soon sound asleep, notwithstanding the restricted dimensions of our couches. Our slumbers were undisturbed, and the night passed without incident.

On the morrow the men who had composed our relief detachment were paraded for inspection by our company commander, Captain Plessier. He addressed us with a few words of welcome, adding some sensible advice concerning the great dangers which existed from sunstroke, fever, and the abuse of alcoholic liquors, and the best way to avoid them. After that he questioned us individually concerning our previous knowledge of building and engineering. Before he interrogated a man, the sergeant-major who stood near him reading from a list he held, would inform our commander of the name and nationality of each in turn. To my surprise he addressed me in very good English, saying:

"What was your profession before you enlisted?"

"I had not yet adopted one, sir," I answered.

"Hum! You evidently possess a good education, and we are in want of intelligent work." Then, turning to the non-commissioned officer behind him, he continued in French: "Sergeant-major! Make a note of it: this man to be put on the brick-making gang in his spare time." As he passed on to the next private he threw a quick glance at me, in which I read a kindly sense of the humour of the situation.

To another who told him he was formerly an artist, he said:

"Excellent! excellent! the very man I want. My hut and the new kitchen will be finished to-morrow, so you can set about whitewashing at once."

This officer was a man of medium height, about thirty-five years of age. He was dark, and wore a small moustache. He was well-built, very active, and seemed to be about at all hours of the day and night. Though a strict disciplinarian he was extremely just, and never inflicted a punishment unless it was merited. Owing to this, and also to his cool courage under fire, his men were devoted to him, and would have followed him anywhere.

The morning was given to us, so as to permit of our settling down in our new quarters.

That afternoon I was initiated into the rudiments of brick-making. The clay pit and yard were at the bottom of the western slope of our position, on the top of which was the réduit or citadel of our little fort. Eight Legionaries were employed at modelling the bricks and stacking them in the kiln (I was one of the gang), and ten native tirailleurs brought water from the well, chopped up the rice straw, and brought in wood for the fire. A picquet of ten men and a corporal, on the watch for snipers, protected us.

We stopped work at 5 p.m., and went up to the fort to take our evening meal, after which I hurried round our positions to take things in, and see all I could before the sun disappeared with that swiftness so startling to the newcomer in the East. In this part of the world there is no twilight.

Again we were favoured with a quiet night. At five o'clock the next morning, just before the bugle sounded the réveil, a sergeant-major came into our abode and gave us the orders for the day. My section, and another from the native regiment, were to start on a morning reconnaissance at six o'clock under the orders of our Captain; the remainder of the garrison was to continue work at the fortifications and buildings in construction. I soon learnt that this was the daily routine, each unit taking alternate turns at reconnoitring or building. A quarter before the hour indicated the section was lined up, outside our pagoda, facing the south gate of the fort.

We were in our khaki kit of cotton drill, and carried our rifles, side arms, 120 rounds of ammunition, water-bottles filled with very weak coffee, and a sort of heavy-bladed half chopper, half knife, which was in a wooden sheath suspended from the belt on the right side. This tool, which is a cross between a Gurkha kookerie and a Manila bolo, is about 18 inches long, and has a blade which is broader and heavier at the end than at the shaft. It is used to cut away the creepers, bamboos, and undergrowth, although at a pinch it makes a formidable weapon. A few minutes later the detachment of native troops who were to take part in the expedition, came from their quarters and formed up behind us. Their uniform, which was of similar texture and shade to ours, consisted of a vest, short trousers, and putties of the same pattern as those worn by the Muong tribes. The men were unshod, and as a head-dress wore a round, flat hat made of bamboo, which is known as a sakalo. This has a diameter of about 8 inches, is painted with red lacquer, and has a small brass spike in the centre. In shape it somewhat resembles an inverted soup-plate. This hat is placed on the top of the chignon-turban worn by the Tonquinese, and secured to it by red cotton streamers. On occasions like the present one, the head-dress was covered by a khaki coiffre, which not only hid the sakalo, but also fell over the neck of each soldier at the back, as a protection from the sun. They were armed with the cavalry musket and bayonet. This weapon was of the same model and calibre as the one we were then using, but it was shorter and lighter. In addition to the native "non-coms" in these regiments each section possessed two French sergeants. These, of course, wore a uniform very much the same as ours.

As I stood in the ranks curiously watching through the trellis-like palisade the red ball of the tropical sun as it rose swiftly above the horizon and lit up the plain before me with colours so brilliant that their glare seemed to burn the eyeball, I overheard the following remarks made by two comrades in proximity to me:

"Himmel! Sidi Mahomet (the sun) promises well to-day. We shall lose some fat before we get back, Bauer."

"Fat! I've none to lose," was the reply. "I found the last of mine in my boots yesterday, when we got back from Yen-Lé (a native village five miles south). That load of bamboo did it. I shall sweat my flesh away now. Pauvre Légion! Have you got a cibiche (cigarette)?"

"That load of bamboo!" said the first speaker, as he handed his chum his pouch. "Do you think I carried back the buthuong's (native headman) feather mattress? Schafskopf! An ironwood pagoda beam, my boy. Eighty kilos, if it weighed a gramme! I heard the Capitän (captain) say, 'This would make splendid doorposts, but it's too heavy,' so I tried it. Sacré nom! It was a blow. When we got here I was nearly dead. Kaput! Sweat? Why, when I went to the kitchen to get a drink of tea, Schmidt stared at me, and asked if it had been raining. Dummer Kerl! The cartridges in my pouch were quite wet. I believe the powder in them must be damp, too."

I joined in the laugh at this sally, and asked:

"Do you know which way we shall go this morning, Bauer?"

"No, I don't," he replied; "and neither does any one else. The 'old man' (le vieux) arranges such matters with himself as he takes his coffee in the morning. All I do know is that if we go south, east or west we shall each bring back a load of bamboo. Mein Gott! It does take a lot to build this place. If we go north we shall have some fun, and some one will probably get hurt."

"No such luck," said the corporal on my right; "there will be no vacancies in the cadre to-day."

As he spoke our Captain came walking down from the réduit, and a few paces behind him one of the buglers leading his mount, a small white native pony, not much bigger than a Shetland, but as beautifully formed as an Arab. Our commander carried no arms; a pair of field glasses slung over his shoulder, and a small malacca cane, constituted all his impedimenta.

He glanced at the detachment, and then said to our lieutenant:

"Monsieur Meyer, the reconnaissance will proceed in the direction of Yen-Lé." (I heard a suppressed groan from the men near me.) "The Tirailleurs will supply the vanguard."

At the word of command one of the native infantrymen left the ranks and went out of the gate at a jog-trot. Once outside, he brought down his rifle from the shoulder, slipped in a cartridge, closed the breech-bolt, and carried his arm at the slope. This man was what is known as the "point" of the column.

When he had proceeded about 40 yards, the "cover-point," composed of a corporal and four men, followed, and behind these, at an equal distance, came the vanguard; which in this case consisted of half a section under the orders of a sergeant. When another interval of 40 yards had been established, the remainder of the column proceeded, with the exception of a small rear-guard of ten men and a corporal, who followed about 100 yards behind us. As we went through the gate, Bauer said to me: "We can be thankful the demoiselles—he meant the native troops—are in front to-day; we shan't have to stretch our skittles (legs)."

Once outside the fort we slung our rifles and marched at ease.

Our road was on a narrow embankment which wound snake-like over the rice fields, and we could only proceed in Indian file.

The country here was very much like that of the Delta, which I have already described. A well-cultivated plain, studded over with villages hidden in clumps of verdure, and surrounded by tall, graceful bamboos, which bent and creaked, and whose delicate foliage rustled under the slightest breeze. The only difference was that here and there were small hills, some covered with long grass, others with a dense and luxuriant vegetation, the pleasant aspect of which broke the monotony of the landscape.

Many of the villages were occupied, and from some of them, as our little column passed by, the notabilities would come out and make obeisance, and offer refreshments to our commander. They had accepted the protection of the French authorities, and paid taxes into the treasury at Phulang-Thuong; but the mere fact that their village was not a mass of charred ruins was the best proof that they must also have been paying toll to De-Nam, and most probably supplying him with rice. Others of these hamlets openly gave proof of their hostility by barring the gates before we arrived. An order would be given and a few men would make a rush for the entrance, pull back the heavy beams placed one above the other, the ends of which fitted in slots cut in two massive posts, and break in the ironwood doors beyond.

No one was found in the place, all the inhabitants having escaped through some exit at the back of the village, generally leading into a dense jungle, where they hid with all the cattle they had time to drive before them.

The defences of these hamlets are much stronger and more elaborate than those of the Delta provinces. A double and sometimes triple embankment and bamboo hedge surrounds them. Between the first two of these are numerous deep ponds of stagnant water. Twisting, narrow lanes, just large enough to allow of the passage of the tame buffalo, divide up the interior,

57

and make of each thick clay-walled house a veritable citadel. Leading up to each of the two or three doors, which must be passed to gain an entrance, are narrow passages through which only one man can go at a time, and these can be raked from end to end by the fire from well-placed loopholes.

I was greatly interested by what I saw that morning, and by the really clever system of defence adopted for their houses by these Asiatics. It is certain that had they offered us any serious resistance we would have suffered severe loss. That they did not, I attribute to the fact that they were fully cognisant that in such a case a gun could be brought from Nha-Nam, against which their fortifications would have stood but a poor chance. As Bauer had predicted, we ended up our morning by bringing back from Yen-Lé a load of bamboo. This we cut from the hedge of that village, which was not inhabited, for it had been burnt about two months previously, because its occupants had fired upon a passing detachment of troops. The task of carrying our load back to Nha-Nam was no light one, and much bad language was used by the way. We reached our position about midday.

Had it been possible to obtain sufficient coolies, the troops would have been spared this labour. However, it did none of us any harm, for we were well fed, and drew a daily ration of a pint of good wine and a lot of rum, so that we could stand a little extra work.

Owing to the extreme heat, unless there was urgent need of their services, the troops were kept under cover each day from 10 a.m. to 2 p.m. From then until near sunset work would be resumed on the buildings and fortifications.

On the 5th May, at 1 a.m., I had my first experience of a night attack. My squad had come off guard-duty on the evening of the 4th, and we had turned in at nine, and were soon fast asleep. White duck pants and a soft linen shirt constituted our usual sleeping costume; each man placing the end of a sheet over his bare feet to protect them from the mosquitoes. In the event of an alarm it was easy for the men to slip on their boots, buckle on their belts, seize their arms and hurry to their posts, of which each was already cognisant. A few seconds sufficed for our little garrison to be prepared to repel any attack on their position. A small light, screened from the outside, burnt in each room, and this prevented the confusion which complete obscurity would have created.

What it was exactly that awoke me it would be difficult to state. Instinctively I had sprung off my cot and was groping about for my boots, which were on the other side of it. After cursing myself for my stupidity, I found and slipped them on. Satisfied at being shod once more—a sense of weakness and inferiority dominates the white man caught barefooted—I did not wait to lace them, but buckled on my belt, took down my rifle from its peg, and hurried over to the opposite side of our pagoda to take up my place at the window, between two other men. But a few seconds had elapsed since my awakening, and now, as I stood with my head and shoulders above the opening, the butt of my rifle pressed under the arm-pit, the right hand gripping the stock with one finger on the trigger, now only did I realise what had brought me from my slumbers. Previously, my awakening intelligence had been able to concentrate itself on one object only, that of arming myself, and reaching my post as soon as possible.

There was no moon, but the night was clear, the stars ablaze. A few yards in front of us I could see the dim outline of the palisade, and, beyond it in the darkness, a grey streak of road which disappeared into the night. Along a front of perhaps 400 yards the sombre background was punctuated again and again, at a distance of about a quarter of a mile, by lightning like red flashes. Rat! tat! tat! tat!... These were Winchesters. Boom! boom!... Sniders or muzzle-loaders. Then Rat! tat! tat! again in quick, continuous succession.

With a sharp whirr, or a long drone, the bullets fly overhead. A swish and a crackle. Ah! that was lower, and has hit the palisade. Thud! Thud! they come into our good wall. A corporal blows out the light; wise man! A crack and a jingle of broken crockery—the tiles of our pagoda are getting it now. Flop! a leaden messenger has come through a window, and flattened itself against the opposite wall.

In our room all is silent. Each man stands with his finger on the trigger; a corporal is behind each squad; we are waiting for orders. In the trenches on the crest of the slope behind us, and in the brick buildings scattered over our position, our comrades, like us, are expectant, ready and confident. The enemy's fire increases, and we hear it break out on the left. The flashes from their rifles come closer and closer; some of them are now not more than 100 yards away.

A good many bullets are finding their way into our building. A tin pannikin, with a hole drilled through it, falls with a clatter from the shelf, and an earthenware jar which contained cold tea is smashed. We can hear the soft trickle of the liquid over the tiled floor.

We take all the cover we can as we peep out into the darkness. No one has been hurt, but it begins to be trying to the nerves.

A ball flicks the window-ledge, and fills our eyes and nostrils with brick-dust. "Schweine!" exclaims my neighbour, rubbing his eyes. "Silence!" says the corporal who stands just behind.

I have a growing desire to say something to somebody, and feel terribly lonely. Next I swear mentally that after counting ten I will open fire and stand all chances. I count ten; then—do nothing, and keep on waiting—it seems for hours. The whole thing lasts about thirty minutes.

At last! We hear footsteps coming down the hill, and Lieutenant Meyer appears walking at a quick pace, a bugler behind him. He comes into our quarters, and looks around in the obscurity to see that all are present. Just then some more of our tiles go to glory with a smash. He laughs lightly, and says:

"Ça chauffe, mes enfants," and a titter runs through the room. Then, turning to a "non-com": "Schmidt! go over to the guard-house" (a few paces away to our left), "and tell the corporal that when the bugle sounds, he will open a fire of six cartridges from the loopholes. You can remain there and join in." Then to us: "Attention! for independent firing! at one hundred metres———"

Every man present braces himself and jubilates. The bugler, at a sign from our officer, steps forward to the doorway and sounds the "Open fire."

In a second we are all at it. Crash! bang! bang! The sentry at the gate also joins in, and we can see the flash and hear the report of his weapon as he fires from behind his shelter of sods.

All my nervous impatience is gone, and I no longer growl at fate and speculate on my chances of being shot in the dark. I am hitting back now, and feel joyful at it. Also I seem to possess two distinct individualities, one watching the other; and the one knows that the other will be pleased if I do not hurry, as I slip another cartridge into the breech, and close the bolt with a snap. So I effect the operation in the regulation manner, though I am craving to rush through it with lightning speed, and would do so, were not my invisible double watching me so attentively. My rifle is as light as a feather as I bring it up to the shoulder. Then I peep along the barrel, and wait a second for a flash from the enemy. It is too dark to see the top sight, so when the flash comes, with a steady pull I loose off at it.

Now the bugle brays the "Cease fire," and the rattling din ceases suddenly.

Within our room all is still again, except for an occasional cough, for we are breathing powder smoke. The place is full of it, and it hangs around like a fog.

The enemy's fire on our front is almost extinct. The little there is comes from a long way off—500 or 600 yards, perhaps. An occasional twinkle and a following pop! and then it ceases altogether.

On the right of our position they are still keeping it up, till we hear the quick successive crashes of two volleys fired by our comrades from the trenches, after which it dies away and is soon finished. So ends the night alarm.

Awaiting orders we remained under arms until our captain came round, accompanied by M. Joly, our surgeon, to enquire if there were any casualties. On our lieutenant replying in the negative, we heard our commanding officer laughingly inform him that the only patient for the doctor was the sergeant-major's dog, which had been shot clean through the body. Strange to say, this animal, a liver-coloured pointer, recovered completely from its wound.

At about a quarter to two the "dismiss" was sounded, and we returned to rest again.

For the next few weeks the work of building went on apace, and by the end of May all the garrison was comfortably lodged and the defences completed. The tirailleurs laboured with us at this task; and it was whilst watching them at work that I was struck by the diversity of uses to which these natives are capable of adapting the bamboo. They used it for almost everything. Roof-beams, doorposts, window frames and rafters were obtained from it for building purposes, and also beds, tables, chairs, matting and blinds. The whole of our position was surrounded by two barriers of bamboo, and in the space between them, about 20 feet, thousands of small pointed stakes of the same wood, boiled in castor oil to harden them, were planted in the ground. The native troops were undoubtedly cunning workmen, and were of great assistance in the construction of the fort.

They are, however, held in small respect by the Legionaries, whose opinion of them as fighters is of the poorest.

The majority of these troops, recruited in the Delta provinces—the population of which are good agriculturists, but possess no military virtues—are of small value as a fighting unit.

The few companies formed of Thos and Muongs (mountain tribes of the Tonquin) have, however, rendered great service to the army, and their courage and morale is of the best.

Unfortunately, only about one-fifth of the total strength of each regiment is composed of these highlanders.

At the beginning of 1891 the colony possessed three regiments of tirailleurs Tonkinois. Each of these corps was composed of four battalions of one thousand men. In June, 1895, a fourth regiment of three battalions was raised, and in 1902 a fifth of similar composition was added to the strength of the army in Tonquin.

Each corps possesses a cadre of French officers and "non-coms," composed as follows: a colonel and an adjutant-major for each regiment, a major to each battalion, and a captain, two lieutenants and twelve sergeants to each company.

There exists, however, a great defect in the organisation of these native corps, of important significance to those acquainted with the admirable system adopted for our Indian army, for not two per cent. of the Frenchmen who compose the cadres of the tirailleurs regiments can speak the vernacular. The disadvantages consequent on this state of things are too evident to require explanation.

CHAPTER IV

Owing to the fact that the majority of the population of the Yen-Thé were partisans of De-Nam, and also to the terror with which this chief had inspired the remainder, it was with the greatest difficulty that any information could be obtained concerning the organisation and movements of the rebels.

Notwithstanding the proverbial cupidity of the natives, and that all intelligence was well paid for—a Special Secret Service fund being devoted to this purpose—the military authorities found it almost impossible to learn what was going on, or what might be expected to happen. It was not until a regular system of espionage was instituted in April, 1891, that any useful knowledge could be obtained.

A score or so of men from the native regiments who had furnished some proofs of courage were chosen, and these, disguised as travelling musicians, beggars or pedlars, wandered from village to village gleaning in the meantime all the information it was possible to obtain. This they would communicate to the officers commanding the forts at Nha-Nam and Bo-Ha, or to the Intelligence Department of the Brigade at Bac-Ninh. These spies were instructed in certain signs and passwords which they used as a proof of their identity when they came to any of the centres with news; and their arrival at and departure from these places were always effected secretly and at night.

By these means it became possible to the French officers to have some idea of what was going on in the lower Yen-Thé, but the knowledge obtained concerning the strength and situation of the rebels' fortified positions in the north was extremely vague.

Several of the spies had made attempts to penetrate into the region north of Ha-Thuong. Some were turned back; others, who had probably excited suspicion, were tortured and decapitated; but none of them succeeded in obtaining a glimpse of the strongholds, or in gaining any certitude concerning the paths which led to them.

However, thanks to these spies, it became known that important convoys of grain and food stuffs, coming from the villages near Bac-Ninh, were sent northwards twice a week, by paths which passed a little to the west of our position, and were not visible from it. The usual time for the passage of these supplies near Nha-Nam was from one to three in the afternoon, at which hour, owing to the heat, the troops were under cover.

Acting on orders received from General Voyron, who had just taken over the command of the 2nd Brigade at Bac-Ninh, small parties were sent out on several occasions in hopes of surprising the convoy.

They were concealed in one of the deserted villages along the paths supposed to be frequented by the rebels, and at points from which a good view of the track for some distance could be obtained. I took part several times in these small expeditions. One of them is perhaps worthy of mention, since it provided some excitement for all those who assisted in it.

Our detachment on this occasion consisted of eight Legionaries, and as many tirailleurs, under the order of a corporal of our regiment. We proceeded due south about 3 miles along the high road to Cao-Thuong to a fine pagoda, the wall of which skirted the highway. Just facing the entrance to the building, and at right angles to the main road which it joined, was a small path that ran across the fields to the west, and was visible for about 400 yards, afterwards turning off sharp to the left behind a range of small hillocks covered with long grass.

At the apex of the angle formed by the junction of this path and the main road was a big banyan tree with a clump of bushes at its base.

It was here that our ambuscade was placed, after a scouting party had gone through a big empty village, situated just behind the pagoda, and it was certain that there existed no sign of occupation, or trace of a recent passage of the enemy.

Six Legionaries, two natives and the corporal remained behind the pagoda wall, and through the open brickwork in the top part of it they could see across the fields. Together with four tirailleurs I was posted on the opposite side of the road. We were a little to the right of the others, our backs towards them, behind the clump of bushes at the foot of the banyan.

Perched up on one of the branches of this tree and concealed by its dense foliage was a Legionary, who, from the position he occupied, obtained a fine view to the south and west: these being the only directions from which our position could be approached, since the bamboo hedge of the village behind us skirted the road to the east for at least 500 yards, and nothing could come from the north without being seen by our sentries at Nha-Nam, who had received orders to keep a sharp look-out.

It was ten in the morning before we had settled down. Our instructions were to reserve our fire, and, if possible, capture one of the enemy alive.

The heat was terrible—this was in the second week in June, and the rains had not broken—and although, thanks to the shade from the tree above me, I could doff my helmet and profit by the occasional light puffs of breeze, just sufficient to move the airy foliage of the bamboo, it required all my energy to fight against the invading drowsiness.

From time to time I would question the man in the tree in the hope that he would announce the advent of a troop; but he disappointed me each time with a reply in the negative.

My attention was soon drawn to the four natives beside me, for I perceived that they were fast asleep. The natives possess a faculty of dropping into a sound slumber without respect to time or position; and these, though seated, their bodies bolt upright and their legs crossed before them, were snoring. The Tonquinese, like the Arabs, have a proverb which says: "A man is better sitting than standing, better asleep than sitting, and better dead than asleep." However, this was no time to ponder on the ethics of Oriental philosophy, so I applied myself to awakening these weary ones, and, after a good deal of vigorous shaking, succeeded in doing so. The corporal, who from his hiding-place had taken in the situation, adjured me, in low but energetic tones, to make use of the butt of my rifle to infuse enthusiasm into the unfortunate tirailleurs. Then all was quiet again, and our weary watching was resumed.

The time seemed to drag along with painful slowness, and the glare and heat increased in intensity. Hardly a sound disturbed the drowsy tranquillity, and had it not been for the chirping song of the cicalas and the far-away whistle of a kite, which soared above us and whose shadow flitted occasionally across the open ground in front, one could have imagined that there was nothing living for miles around.

The sun began to move westwards, and its rays struck the white wall behind me, only to be reflected with such force that I was obliged to put on my helmet to protect the back of my head. It was nearly two in the afternoon when we were startled by a short exclamation from the sentry perched above us.

"What is it?" somebody enquired.

"There is something moving," he replied, "a long way off—two kilomètres, perhaps—two men—Ah! there are some who carry baskets. Nhaques (peasants) going to market, I suppose." Then with growing excitement in his tone he continued: "I see a glitter. Got for deck!" (he was a Belgian). "The two men in front carry rifles—they are the point! Yes! Yes! the point! Further back there are more coolies with baskets, and more men with rifles—now two men on ponies."

"Where are they?" I tried to speak quietly, but could have shouted with excitement.

"On the path which runs behind the hillocks—the path which turns in here. They come from the south, and walk very quickly. Wheew!" he whistled, "there are quite sixty coolies, and as many men with guns. They have a rear-guard. The first will be on the path before us in ten minutes. Prévenez vite le caporal—Nous allons rire!"

I ran across the road behind us, through the gateway into the pagoda yard, and informed our "non-com." Though he was only half awake when I began—for the heat had been too much for him—he was quite alive to the situation before I had said many words, and almost shook hands with me in his joy at the news.

"Don't shoot," he said, "unless they are alarmed and run, then shoot straight. Let them come up on the road here and we can collar one, mais pour l'amour de Dieu! Keep an eye on your demoiselles—I have no faith in them!"

I went back to my hiding-place. Hellincks, the man in the tree, said to me:

"Hurry up! The two first will be round the corner in a minute or so."

I glanced at the tirailleurs. They were kneeling now, and throwing eager glances through the foliage. In a low voice I told them to fix bayonets and load, and noticed that the man next to me trembled like a leaf as he did so. Excitement, I thought—or was it fear? From a deep bronze his skin had changed to a dirty yellow. I should have known and taken away his weapon, but this was my first experience.

Mechanically I slipped my right hand into the pouch of my belt, took out a cartridge, and after wetting the bullet with my tongue, slipped it into the open breech of my rifle and closed it. Now nothing moved, and the only sounds that struck the ear were the song of the cicalas, the whistle of the kite, and the gentle rustle of the bamboos in the breeze.

Suddenly, round the corner of the last hillock, came a man; then, a yard or so behind, another. Though expected, their actual appearance produced an impression of surprise; perhaps because we had waited so long.

Both wore a kind of uniform of green cotton cloth, and putties of the same colour. Their long hair was rolled in a silken turban of similar hue. Hanging on his shoulders, suspended by a string which passed round the front of his neck, each man had a big palm-leaf hat.

The sun glittered on their brass cartridges fixed in a belt round the waist, and on the Winchesters which they carried on the shoulder, as a gardener carries his spade; the end of the muzzle in the hand, the butt behind them.

On they came at a sort of jog-trot, and we could hear the pad! pad! pad! of their naked feet on the hot path.

Now they were within 100 yards of us, and I fancied I could perceive a look of relief on the ugly flat features of the first as he glanced towards the pagoda.

The first of the long string of bearers with their bamboo and baskets were now visible, coming along at a jerky run. I felt something touch my left elbow, and glanced round to find that Hellincks had come down from his perch and was kneeling beside me.

The two armed men were quite near now. We could see a bead of perspiration on the face of the first as it came from his hair and trickled down his forehead. We could hear the regular, short pant of his hard breathing, note his half-open mouth, and distinguish his black-lacquered teeth.

Pad! pad! pad!—a soft puff of breeze brought to my nostrils the acrid odour of the perspiring native. Another few seconds, and by thrusting my rifle through the leaves I could have touched his breast with the muzzle.

These two will surely be ours; nothing can save them!

Unable to control himself, mastered by excitement or fear, the tirailleur on my right suddenly sprang to his feet, and shouted in the vernacular:

"Toi!" ("Stop!") "Adow di?" ("Where go you?")

From the pagoda behind us I heard an angry murmur, and could distinguish the corporal's voice: "Kill the swine! Oh, kill him!"—Hellincks cursed and groaned like a man struck with fever. I felt that I had stopped sweating, and a big lump rose from my chest into my throat, and seemed to choke me. I gave a great sob of disappointment and surprise.

The next instant we were on our feet, for Hellincks rose with me, and as he shouted, "We can yet catch one," I knew that he had a similar thought to mine. But we had hardly taken the first step forward, prior to forcing our way through the bushes and jumping down into the paddy field, than we were blinded for a second by two bright flashes from a few feet in front of us, and half deafened by the close report of the rebels' Winchesters. The linh (native soldier), the cause of all the racket, pitched head foremost into the foliage. There was no time to lose, so both of us rushed through the little cloud of smoke, through the bushes, and the next instant we were down in the field.

Fifteen, perhaps twenty, yards away I saw the backs of the two green-clad natives who were running for dear life. They were side by side in the field, for the path was littered with the baskets and bamboos of the coolies, who had disappeared as if by magic. "Too late!" I shouted. Hellincks jerked up his rifle and covered the native on the left. The next instant, acting on his example, I was peeping along my sights and bringing them in line on to the middle of the palm-leaf hat, which bumped as it hung on the receding back of the man to the right.

Before I could press the trigger Hellincks had fired, and a cloud of smoke floated across my line of vision. It was gone in a second, and I got my chance. Through the white puff from my rifle I saw a dark figure spring into the air with the pose of a marionette of which all the strings have been jerked together; and, as I brought down my weapon, jerked out the empty cartridge and reloaded, I saw a dark mass lying motionless on the damp ground amongst the bright green stalks of young rice.

"Vite! vite! you fool, mine is winged, and will escape if you do not hurry!" cried my comrade, as he started off at the double.

On we ran for about 30 yards; then Hellincks stopped, and, pointing to the ground, jerked out: "I told you so"; and I saw a small blotch the size of a man's hand, which, as the bright sunshine played upon it, glittered red like a splendid dark ruby.

"These fellows have as many lives as a cat," he continued hurriedly. "He was down and up again in a second; limped away across the path into that tall grass on the right"—pointing in that direction. "Come! we may yet have him."

On we went a few more yards, when the Belgian came a cropper, having tripped over the foot of the thing spread-eagled in the rice field. In his hurry he had passed too close. I had given it a wide berth. I came back to help him up, and had to look at it. There was a small round hole in the back of the neck, just below the base of the skull.

Hellincks scrambled up, panting. How he cursed!

"What are you staring at, man? Take his gun—quick!"

Bending down, I picked up the Winchester. In doing so I almost touched the body, and with difficulty suppressed a murmured, "I beg your pardon," because I was dominated by a sentiment of awesome respect for the thing that had been, and was no more. I wished to walk softly, on tiptoe, and felt so thankful that he had fallen face-downwards.

All this had passed in the space of a few seconds. "Come back! come back!" It was the corporal shouting to us, and there was a note of warning in his voice.

Before turning to go I glanced up, and saw a puff of white smoke arise, float for a second over the top of the hillock ahead, and I heard a report. Something struck the wet ground a little in front and to my right. A speck of mud hit me on the chin; then, along a distance of 50 yards or so, the crest was covered with smoke, and there was a rattle of musketry.

As we ran the ground and the air seemed to me to be alive, and I could not go quickly enough to please myself.

Hellincks said between pants: "We forgot the cartridges."

"Oh! d—- the cartridges!" I replied, and it was as if some one else had said it.... How far it seemed!—there were not more than 40 yards. How hot the sun was! I believe I was terribly afraid during the few seconds it took us to get back to shelter again.

How we got back I don't remember; I only know that I felt quite surprised to find myself standing, somewhat blown, behind the big tree, telling my "non-com" what had happened, and feeling very anxious not to appear flustered.

Hellincks lay panting and laughing on the grass beside the other men—three Legionaries, who were making caustic remarks concerning our running powers, and five tirailleurs. The latter were either kneeling sheltered by the tree, or extended flat on the road, their rifles ready to reply to the enemy's fire, which was increasing in intensity.

To my explanation the corporal replied:

"Bon! bon! It was the fault of that dog of a native. Pity he was not hit—killed. They shot off his sakalo, and he fainted. Three of our fellows and two tirailleurs are behind the pagoda wall to the right; they can see the enemy's position from there. Go and take command of them" (I was an élève-caporal—i.e., lance-corporal—at this time), "and follow up each volley we fire from here by another—distance, 300 yards."

I went over to my little command, my nerves steadied by the thought of the responsibility which was now mine.

I lined the men up, each before an aperture in the open brickwork of the wall, and recommended them to aim carefully, and wait for the word of command before firing.

Half sitting, half lying, with his head against the wall, was the tirailleur who had been the cause of our abortive ambuscade. The upper half of his face was scorched and blackened, and a little red stream trickled down from forehead to chin. He looked dazed and stupid, and his eyes were half closed. From his lips came a continual moan, which he interrupted every few seconds to murmur: "Tiet! Tiet!" ("Dead! Dead!")

My attention was called from him by the crash of a volley from the corporal's party.

As soon as the smoke had risen the smart rattle of our volley rang out. Three times I gave the same commands, and each detonation seemed an echo to the one from the rifles of our comrades. Then there was a pause.

The enemy's fire had slackened considerably, and the noise of the projectiles as they struck the wall and roof of the pagoda, sang overhead or clattered through the branches of the banyan, was hardly noticeable when compared to the racket they had kept up a few minutes before. From the hillocks before us only occasional puffs of smoke arose, followed by isolated reports from their rifles.

At his call I went out to our "non-com," who said:

"They seem to be sick of it, and certainly show no disposition to rush us. I wish they would try, Sacré bleu! The ground is too open for them. If we could depend on the linhs—but we can't—we might make a dash for the convoy; without them the odds are too great, so I have decided to withdraw. I will start off with this lot. When we have got away give them a volley to keep them still; and if they show any signs of moving, a little independent firing. Don't be extravagant, though. You understand?"

"Yes," I answered. "But you must take that wounded linh; he would hamper me."

"Of course," he replied. "Sacré bon Dieu! I had forgotten the coward. Can he stand?"

"I don't think so."

Thereupon he told two men off to fetch the poor beggar, and I felt sorry for him when he appeared tottering, though supported by the two Legionaries.

As already explained, the banyan tree and the bushes masked the pagoda gateway, so that these movements could not be seen by the enemy.

"He'll do," said the corporal. "You two men hold on to him, and help him to keep up. Here you"—this to another tirailleur—"tell him to run his best when we go."

This was explained; and he nodded, mumbled, and would have started off alone if he had not been held. He seemed in a hurry to get away, and we all laughed.

"Now," said our chief, "the Brigade will retire by echelons." Then, with a grin and a bow to me: "You, monsieur, will cover our withdrawal with your battalion. When you hear a volley from us, double out and rejoin with your party. Good luck to you!"

"Bonne chance!" I replied, and went back to my men.

A couple of sharp orders, and the others clattered by at the double. The next minute the enemy's fire broke out with renewed vigour. They probably thought that everybody had left, for no bullets came our way.

Crash! went our volley at them, but they still kept it up: the running white men were too tempting a target.

I waited half a minute, and ordered independent firing of four cartridges per man, and joined in the fun.

This calmed them a little, and I got my men outside, sheltered behind the friendly banyan, ready for the run, as it was probable that the others would soon halt.

The road went off slightly to the right, and was hidden from view by the corner of the wall. We had not long to wait, for in a few seconds the rattle of the rifles told me it was time to start, so away we went in single file at the run. We found the first detachment sheltered behind a ridge between two fields, from whence they had fired two volleys to cover our withdrawal. No one had been hit, the only damage done being to the stock of a rifle belonging to a man who had retreated with me, which had been smashed by a rifle bullet.

There can be no doubt that the rebels were very poor shots at anything over 100 yards; and it is doubtful if any of them knew how to hit a running object. It was not for us to grumble at this, however.

Their fire ceased completely, as soon as we had joined forces. This was due, probably, to the fact that, owing to the continued sound of firing, the picquet from Nha-Nam had been sent out to meet us—though we were unaware of this, as a slight rise of the ground hid the fort from us. We moved off cautiously, and very soon met the relief. This detachment, about fifty strong, went on in hope of engaging the enemy, but were disappointed; for, although they occupied the hillocks from which we had been fired upon, the rebels had not waited for them but retreated, together with the convoy, leaving behind them but a few baskets of rice. So terminated my first experience under fire from a visible enemy.

That night we were awakened, and remained under arms for an hour, for the enemy amused themselves by treating us to a long range fire. It was a waste of ammunition, for nobody was hurt, and we did not reply. Some of my comrades suggested that this was a reprisal for our ambuscade of the afternoon. Personally, I am inclined to believe that it was a feinted attack on our position, designed to engage our attention, and ensure the passage of the belated convoy which had escaped us.

The weather now grew hotter every day, and several cases of heat, apoplexy and fever occurred in our little garrison. It is probable that the fever was due to the digging which had taken place during the construction of our fortifications. This was inevitable, of course; but it is always very dangerous to break new soil in these districts, since the surface to the depth of 3 or 4 feet is mainly composed of decayed vegetation in which the malaria microbe is abundant.

All the newcomers were, of course, victims to prickly-heat, in addition to which many of us were afflicted with small boils. These would not come one or two at a time, but sufferers were literally covered with them. I was one of the first to pay toll to this extremely painful malady. In addition to these unavoidable inconveniences, the whole company suffered from another discomfort which was a cause of deep complaint on the part of the men, since it was due to the neglect of our commissariat department. Because some trifling formality had not been executed, mosquito-nets were not served out to us till late in July, and the lack of them caused many hours of sleepless agony during the hot nights.

A surprising amount of red-tapeism still remained in the commissariat department of France's colonial army; and, though this branch was remodelled at the beginning of 1901, it is generally acknowledged that the authorities responsible for the new order of things have obtained little or no improvement in this respect.

In July the heat became tremendous; the afternoons, which were the hottest part of the day, averaging 110 degrees in the shade. The men were kept indoors from nine in the morning until three in the afternoon, and operations were restricted to short reconnaissances, which took place either in the early morning or in the evening.

These excursions were always made to the south, east or west, but not northwards, as orders had been received from the Brigade to abstain from penetrating into the enemy's country until the summer months had passed. In consequence, the garrison of Nha-Nam disposed of a good deal of leisure time, which the men made use of according to their varied tastes.

Making cloth belts embroidered with flags and other warlike devices was a favourite pastime with many; books and newspapers were in great demand, and a fortnightly convoy from Phulang-Thuong, which brought the European mail, was an incident of importance to all. A rifle range had been built about 500 yards to the west of our position, and each morning saw some unit of the garrison at practice.

Close to the fort, on the south-west side, was a small village inhabited by the camp followers, wives and children of some of the native troops. It contained one small store kept by a Chinaman, at which the troops could obtain tobacco, tinned goods, and strong drinks.

The sale of intoxicants was, however, subjected to strict regulation, any infringement of which would have entailed the peremptory closing of the storekeeper's establishment. The men not on duty were allowed to go into the village from 5 to 7 p.m. only, so that would-be topers had small facilities for over-indulgence, and cases of drunkenness were few and far between. Thirsty souls could obtain good wine from the Government stores in the fort at a very reasonable price, though this supply was with reason restricted to half a litre (a little more than a pint) a day per man.

Our diet was good, for the natives from some of the surrounding villages brought in a plentiful supply of eggs, poultry, pork, fruit and yams, which were readily purchased, as the troops received a mess-grant in addition to their daily ration of bread, fresh meat, coffee, sugar, rice and salt.

During the period of comparative inaction, and profiting by the leisure at my disposal, I made an attempt at learning the Annamese language. Progress was very slow, for the vernacular, like Chinese, is composed of a multitude of sounds, many of which are so similar to each other that only a well-trained ear can distinguish the difference; also, there exists neither alphabet nor grammar to aid the student, and success depends entirely on the possession of a good memory, and inexhaustible patience.

In writing this language the natives use the Chinese characters, each representing a sound; and the extent of knowledge of their literati class is gauged by the number of these each individual has succeeded in retaining. Thus a native who has passed examinations which prove that he possesses five thousand characters, is said to be clever; and one who has shown that he can make use of double that quantity is considered to have reached a very high standard of education indeed.

As in the Chinese and Japanese languages many words possess an honorific as well as a common form. Thus an official, in speaking to an inferior, will refer to himself by using the word tao (I); but in conversing with a superior this form of pronoun in the first person becomes toy (I). It is needless to state that this peculiarity adds considerably to the difficulties the student has to reckon with.

During my search for an insight into the native tongue I came in contact with one of the native sergeants, known as Doy-Tho (doy—sergeant, and tho—a mountaineer). This non-commissioned officer belonged to the hardy and brave mountain tribes of Northern Tonquin, mention of which has already been made.

He had distinguished himself on several occasions, and especially so during the operations against Hou-Thué in December and January.

In appearance, and in his love of danger, he bore a strong resemblance to a Gurkah; and the following account of an incident which took place during one of the attacks on the rebel stronghold, related to me by a Legionary who was present, will give the reader some insight into the character of this plucky little soldier, and indeed into that of his fellow-tribesmen, of whom he was a good example.

During one of the first engagements a section of the native regiment under the orders of a lieutenant succeeded in reaching the first palisade. From behind the trees, or lying flat on the ground, the men opened a smart fire on the rebel position, which was returned with vigour and punctuated by

Oriental abuse, composed of rude remarks concerning the individual family of each tirailleur, and the graves of his ancestors.

Doy-Tho, maddened by these insults, stood up in full view of the enemy, and poured forth upon them a torrent of curses and invective.

In their admiration of his daring, and their surprise at the volubility and scope of his abuse, most of the combatants forgot to fire, and a momentary lull took place in the engagement. It lasted a few seconds only, for, lashed to fury by the stinging retorts of the speaker, every rifle on that side of the rampart was turned upon him.

His sakalo and cartridge-cases were shot away, and his clothes riddled with bullet holes; and it is probable that his body would have resembled a sieve had not his lieutenant sprung forward and dragged the howling mountaineer into safety behind a big tree. After this the rebels' fire slackened, and they shouted friendly invitations to the native troops to kill their officers and join them, saying that De-Nam would treat them well, and give one hundred dollars for every head of a French officer they would bring in.

Tho replied with renewed invective from behind the tree, where he had been ordered to remain, and each pause, made through want of breath, he punctuated with a shot from his rifle.

When the engagement was over, and the troops were retiring to Nha-Nam, the lieutenant aforementioned asked the little sergeant if he thought the promises of the rebels were bona fide ones. The nearest translation of Doy-Tho's reply in bad French was something after the following:

"Hum! they belong big liars. Suppose I bring your head, mon lieutenant, perhaps I get ten dollars only."

He and I soon became fast friends, and of an evening, before the door of the fort was closed, I would sometimes go for an hour to his caigna (native hut), and sit and talk with him whilst his wife prepared his evening meal of rice, dried fish, prawns and native salad.

While we discussed the topics of the day, his sons—two sturdy, pot-bellied brats, aged respectively five and seven, naked as they were born—would squat down on the floor of beaten clay and stare open-mouthed at me.

His meal despatched, the little sergeant would stretch himself out on a clean rice straw mat placed on a platform-like bed made of split bamboo which covered half the room. His wife would then bring in a hardwood tray, whereon was a diminutive lamp, a bamboo opium pipe with a blue clay bowl, some little skewer-like implements of silver, and a tiny box of the same metal containing the daily ration of this seductive drug.

Tho would lie on his right side, a hollow block of green-enamelled earthenware, serving as a pillow, beneath his head. His wife would stretch out opposite to and facing him. Between them was placed the tray with its little implements, and the lamp was lit.

This was the solemn moment of the day.

Tho reached out his skinny little brown hand and picked up his pipe, fondling it an instant prior to warming the bowl in the flames, his keen black eyes glancing over his favourite with the fond look of satisfaction and gratitude one sees on the face of a man who greets a well-beloved wife.

This pipe, if such it can be called (for neither in bowl nor stem did it resemble the instrument we give that name to), was of similar form to that used by all Orientals who inhale opium fumes. It consisted of a stem, about 2 feet long, of polished bamboo, about 1½ inches in diameter, the lower end being closed by an ivory cap, while the other extremity was covered by a disc of silver with a small round hole in the centre of it. To this the lips were placed when the fumes were inhaled.

About 6 inches from the lower end of the stem the bamboo was pierced to receive the neck of the bowl, shaped like a hollow, flat bulb. The top had a diameter of about 3 inches, and was well polished and slightly convex. In the middle was a tiny hole about as big as a pin's head.

It is, perhaps, as well to explain that no opium gets into the bowl, for it is consumed over the hole in the smooth convex surface on the top, owing to the air in the bulb having been inhaled and the consequent creation of a temporary vacuum. Thus only the fumes pass through the little orifice, up the stem and into the lungs of the smoker.

Now Tho was warming his pipe over the flame of the lamp, withdrawing it now and again to gently polish the surface of the bulb upon the sleeve of his khaki jacket. His better-half dipped one of the little silver skewers into the tiny pot, and after turning it round drew it out covered with a coating of the rich brown drug, which looked like thick treacle.

This she held over the flame for a second. It frizzled and gained in consistency; she withdrew it, and dipped it again into the drug, and it increased in volume. Three or four times this operation was repeated, until there was sufficient opium on the skewer to make a good pipe.

The Doy now held his pipe to his mouth, and the tip of the flame licked the smooth, warm surface of the bowl on which his spouse began to roll the opium, holding the other end of the pipe in her left hand to steady it.

Her dexterity was marvellous. In a few seconds the drug was detached from the skewer, and was rolled into a little ball about the size of a pea.

She threw a glance at Tho which meant, "Are you ready?" He nodded, and started drawing at the bamboo. A gentle movement, and the skewer pushed the ball of opium on to the tiny hole, and it was held just over the lamp.

There was a frizzle as the drug began to burn, continuing under the steady prolonged suction of the smoker. There was no smoke, for it was all going up the pipe into the little brown man's lungs. His eyes were half closed, and his features expressed a gentle beatitude, but his chest was swelling, swelling. Soon he could not continue the steady suction, and he drew at the bamboo with a succession of quick, small pants. His wife, in the meanwhile, held the bowl well over the flame, and pushed up to the orifice the tiny particles of the drug still adhering to the convex surface. Presently all was consumed. I, on seeing this for the first time, sighed with relief, as one who had escaped from witnessing a catastrophe, when the smoker opened his mouth, and allowed the black smoke to escape slowly from between his lacquered teeth, which shone like ebony in the dim light of the tiny lamp.

Tho watched the opaque column as it climbed slowly upwards to the bamboo cross-poles of his hut, and, forming into a little cloud, clung to the thatch of the roof. "Biet!" (good) he exclaimed, and then prepared for another.

The air in the tiny room was now heavy with the odour of the drug, which at first seemed acrid and unpleasant, but it improved on acquaintance, and soon became soothing and enjoyable.

The Doy liked to smoke his opium in peace, and, knowing this, I sat waiting until he should see fit to break the silence. Outside, the day was fast drawing to a close, and the short eastern sunset would in a few minutes be changed into night.

From the Chinaman's shanty a few paces away came the sound of a rollicking ditty sung by some of my comrades over a pint of wine or a glass of absinthe. The noise seemed to wake all the cicalas in the neighbourhood, for they started at once a concert of chirping whistles. In the half-dried-up pools outside the village thousands of noisy members of the batrachian tribe broke into an endless chorus of complaint at the unwonted dryness of the season, while from time to time their big uncles, the bull-frogs, added a booming croak of approval. The matting hanging before the doorway of the hut swung back a little, moved by a hot breeze which brought to the nostrils a whiff of flowers and vegetation in decay; and I could see the fireflies already circling down the little street or about the thatch-covered caignas.

The heat was terrific, and seemed, if possible, less supportable now than it had done during the hours of blinding, scorching sunshine. All the earth seemed to radiate the caloric it had been stoking up during the day.

When would the rains break? Those rains the other men who knew had told me of. Rains that chilled you to the bone, and made your teeth chatter.

The thought that in the past—it seemed years ago—I had somewhere shivered with the cold, made me laugh aloud, as, after throwing off my light cotton jacket and rolling up my shirt-sleeves, I sat mopping the perspiration from my forehead. The veins of my neck seemed to swell, and my breath came in gasps.

Thinking that it might be somewhat cooler there, I stepped into the street, and taking out my pouch, tried to roll a cigarette. Three times the thin paper broke in my sticky, perspiring fingers before I succeeded in obtaining a damp and flabby apology for a smoke. This slight exertion had caused me to perspire from every pore, and it seemed hotter outside than within. My light clothes clung to my limbs like those of a man pulled out of a pond. Disgusted, I returned and sat down again on the edge of the bed, and, after endless difficulty, succeeded in lighting my damp cigarette with a still damper match.

The tiny twinkle of the opium-lamp deepened the darkness outside the small circle of its light. Tho's brownish-yellow features, on which it shone, reminded me of a quaint and clever old Japanese ivory I had once seen; and the dark background of the night was like the black velvet-lined case which had contained it.

From where I sat I could see the arm of the sergeant's wife—bare from the elbow—and I watched with a kind of sleepy fascination her small and nimble fingers as they manipulated the drug. The soft light gave to her skin a rich gold tint, and made the arm and hand look graceful and comely. The Rembrandt-like effect of the picture gripped me, and for the moment the heat was forgotten.

Tho's voice brought me from a waking dream when, after laying down his pipe, he said:

"Patience, camarade! It will come. When the bull-frogs join in the song the great waters are not far off. Were you on sentry to-night you would hear the dreary note of the rain-bird, for I'd stake a week's pay she will be out. Ba (his wife) tells me it sang to-day before sunrise; but women were ever dreamers."

The little woman looked up from her task of cleaning the silver skewer, and retorted:

"Dreamers! Oh, great slaughterer of men, and dost thou give me time to dream? Is not my life as full of work as our mountain rise is full of fat? Am I not still a tho from the Tam-Dao? (a group of mountains to the west of Thaï-Nguyen). Are not my teeth white, though I have a husband who has blackened his and become a plainsman?"

As she smiled at her own wit I caught a flash of ivory between her red lips, and noticed for the first time the regularity of her small features. The Doy smiled good-naturedly, and replied:

"Oh, thou silly one! Thou art pretty as an angry parrakeet, and talkest faster." Then to me: "Had I not lacquered my poor teeth—though my ancestors know the grief I suffered from it—how could I have gone, dressed like a pedlar, to spy in the villages for the Government? Had I tried so to do, the De-Nam would have eaten my liver long since. As it is, some day I shall probably eat his. Ba, get ready another pipe for me."

"Nay! nay!" she answered, as she lit a small kerosine lamp of German make, and placed it on the bed; "thou hast eaten ten times of the drug, and it is thy just ration." She blew out the small light and carried away the tray, saying to me as she did so: "Were I to listen to this man he would turn all the Government dollars he gets into black smoke, and I and my sons would have to go in shame to my father and beg for food."

It was very evident that Madame Ba ruled the roost, and it was probably better so.

Tho growled a little, and protested to me:

"Was ever man burdened with such a wife? She has no respect for me—the senior sergeant in the company. Now, had I married——" Here he was interrupted by the first notes of the bugle calling us back to the fort, and we rose together and hurried out of the hut. It was quite dark outside. Tho did not speak until we had nearly reached the gate, then he said: "Camarade, when the time comes, I hope you will find for yourself a white woman with a heart like Ba's. Bonne nuit!" And he ran off to his section.

Lying on my bed that night I communicated to my neighbour, Lipthay, a Hungarian, the incidents of the evening, and together we laughed over the recital of little Tho's domestic worries. This room-mate of mine had come out with our detachment on the Bien-Hoa. On our arrival at Nha-Nam we had been given beds next each other, and our acquaintance was fast ripening into a close friendship.

Lipthay had joined in April of the preceding year. Shortly before this he held a commission in the Austrian army, which he had resigned. A braver, more loyal and upright nature I have never met. I have never learnt the reasons which brought him into the Legion, but am convinced they were honourable, for during the four years we were almost continually together his speech and conduct were always those of a gentleman in the truest sense of the word.

He was an adept at military topography, and, to while away the time, would give me further lessons in this useful art, of which I had already some slight knowledge.

This having reached the ears of our Captain, we accompanied in turns the occasional reconnoitring parties, and made topos of the route taken. His work was of the first quality, and his draughtsmanship of a very high order.

The following morning I came across Tho, who was conducting the sick men of his detachment to the doctor. He halted an instant to ask me if I was coming to see him that evening, and I told him I should be deprived of that pleasure, as my section was on picquet duty at 5 p.m. At this he grinned, and said:

"Well, then, we shall meet later, for there will be some fun to-night." He then left me, and trotted off to rejoin his men.

I knew it was no good trying to obtain further information from him, for the Doy was like the majority of Orientals, from whom torture will not wring a secret they have decided to keep, so I did not attempt to see him again that day.

However, as I knew that he served as interpreter to our commander when spies were interrogated, I inferred from the hint he had given me that some movement was to be made that night.

My section assembled, and were inspected with the guard that evening, and afterwards we were dismissed, but had to remain dressed and armed in our room in the event of our services being required. I took Lipthay into my confidence, and told him of the "tip" I had received. I induced him to do as I did, and fill his water-bottle with cold coffee in case of necessity.

Fully dressed, with our belt and cartridge-cases on, we lay down on our cots to snatch a few hours' rest. At 1 a.m. our squad corporal shook us out of our slumbers, and, together with the other men of our section, we snatched up our rifles and assembled outside as quietly as possible.

Here we found a half-section of native troops under the orders of Tho, who nodded to me and grinned as I stepped up and took my place in the ranks. Two hard-boiled eggs and a slice of bread were served out to each man, which we were told to put in our wallet for future use.

A few minutes later Captain Plessier came upon the scene, and noticing that he was not mounted, I surmised that our coming peregrinations were to take place over difficult ground.

So indeed it proved, for, after the gate had been opened by the sentry, our little column went out in silence, like a troop of ghosts, in Indian file, turned to the right, and proceeded to the south-west across the paddy fields by the narrow ridges which served as paths.

The night was stifling and pitch-dark—so dark, indeed, that each man had to hold on to the wallet of his comrade in front so as not to lose his way. Thus progress was very slow. When we had been walking about an hour, and had covered, perhaps, a mile and a half, the blackness of the night was of a sudden lit up by a brilliant flash of lightning which illuminated, for the fraction of a second, the surrounding country. The weird aspect of it, with the tall outlines of the palms and bamboo silhouetted against the sky, remained with a strange vividness as if photographed upon the retina, for sevseveral minutes. This was succeeded by a peal of thunder so deafening that it seemed to split the ear-drums and shake the ground beneath us, and the rain came down as it only can do in the tropics.

For a few seconds our little troop was thrown into confusion, and some of the men, temporarily blinded by the sudden light, stepped into the fields, where they floundered about with water and mud almost up to their knees. After this interruption we proceeded on our way.

Very slowly though, for the lightning continued, flash following flash, in quick succession for an hour, and our ears were weary with the crashing of the thunder. The track, which was of clay, was sodden and slippery. We were all wet through to the skin, and our boots, full of water, emitted a curious squashing noise at each step.

Fortunately the din of the thunder and the continued thresh of the rain more than covered the noisy advance of our column.

Ten minutes before, wet through with perspiration, I had mentally cursed the heat; now my teeth were chattering and my fingers were numbed with the cold. I felt a strange joy at it, smiled to myself at the evident truth of Tho's recent prophecy anent the "great waters," and thought how appropriate was his term for the downpour.

For two hours we continued on our slippery way, and were then halted on a patch of grass covered with little mounds—a village graveyard.

Here our expedition was broken up into little parties, the one to which I belonged being composed of ten Legionaries and a sergeant, and as many tirailleurs, with Tho at their head.

We proceeded a short distance, and were ordered to be down in some long grass, behind a clump of cactus and hibiscus shrubs. As we did so, I heard the Doy say to our sergeant:

"When it will be light we shall see the door of the village from here; the path to it is a little to our left."

From this, and the movements I could hear on our right and left, I gathered that the remainder of the column was surrounding a village which lay before us, but owing to the darkness and the rain I could distinguish nothing ahead of me.

We had been lying on the ground some minutes, and, notwithstanding the chill dampness, I was almost falling into a doze, for the walk had tired me, when from the surrounding darkness a figure came noiselessly and crouched beside me. The next instant Tho's voice whispered in my ear:

"I told you so; it has come."

"Yes"—I shivered—"and I think I have had enough of it."

"No! say not so! A few more hours and you will grumble at the heat once more, camarade! 'Tis a fool who ever complains. Our land had sore need of the rain; the crops will drink this as the mandarin does his Yunan tea. When the sun rises all the earth will rejoice. The voice of the tempest has shut the ears of our enemy to the noisy approach of the linhtap lanxa (European soldier). This time we shall surely surprise the brigands; therefore we should thank our Lord Bhouddah for his great mercy."

"What village is before us, friend?"

"Yen-Trieu," he answered; "and in it is a linh-binh (sergeant) of the De-Nam with twenty men. They are collecting the taxes, and were to have left it this morning. But they will never leave it," he added, with a low chuckle. "Yesterday the spies came and told the Captain. I was there. Last night they surely feasted, drank much choum-choum (rice alcohol), and smoked many pipes, for the headman is a great traitor, and in secret a partisan of Ham-Nghi."

"We shall have much trouble to enter," I ventured, "for we have not brought axes."

Tho chuckled again, and said:

"Let not that trouble thee. I have advised the Ong-quang-Ba (the Captain—literally, 'Lord of three stripes'), and these fools will open the door themselves; even as I said to him."

I turned to chide him for his presumption, but he had glided away silently into the night.

The rain had ceased now almost as suddenly as it had commenced, and the smell of the damp earth and vegetation reeked in the nostrils. Turning, I glanced behind me, and saw that towards the east the sky was grey. In a few minutes the forms of my comrades near by could be dimly distinguished. The nearest—he was barely a yard away—was a boy of twenty, an Alsatian. He was fast asleep, his head pillowed on his arm, and dreaming pleasantly, for on his lips, which bore no trace of a moustache, I could discern a smile. Fearing lest the sergeant should find him thus, I awoke him, and he thanked me.

It was now so light that a few paces away to the left I recognised our Captain, seated on the ground. He was chewing the end of an unlit cigar. In a low voice he called the sergeant, and talked for some moments to him.

Then our "non-com" came from one to the other of us and communicated the instructions he had just received. These were:

"Load, and fix bayonets as quietly as possible. Lie still until the signal is given by the Captain with his whistle, then rise at once and rush for the village gateway, and on into the houses beyond; weapons not to be used until resistance is offered; and every effort must be made to capture an enemy alive."

By looking through the foliage before us, we could now see in the yet dim light that we were close to a pond or moat, covered with rank duckweed and lotus plants. On the other side of this was a big village, surrounded by the usual embankment and bamboo hedge. Presently we could hear the crowing of cocks, barking of dogs, and other sounds of awakening life.

The pond was crossed by a dyke about 6 feet wide, forming a path leading to the heavy gateway of the hamlet. This was yet closed.

By this time the eastern sky was a bright red violet, and against it the great leaves of the plantains, the spiky foliage of the macaw palms, and the delicate leafage of the bamboo seemed to be cut out of tinfoil, reminding me of a tropical scene from a drama staged in one of our large London theatres. The birds were out: troops of white-breasted jays scurried from tree to tree, with an uncouth cry; sparrows darted about with an endless twittering; and several carrion-crows started a concert among the areca palms inside the village. Suddenly on the horizon there was a glitter, and a convex curve of fire appeared. The mighty ball of the blinding sun rose inch by inch from the rice fields, the wet surface reflecting its light with dazzling vividness.

It was already hot, and our sodden linen grew stiffer and drier each instant.

All attention was now turned to the village, and behind the gate came the noise of withdrawal of bolts and bars. The heavy ironwood portals swung open, and out stepped a water-buffalo, on whose back straddled a naked youngster, gripping tightly a cord attached to the iron ring in the animal's nostrils. Just outside the unwieldy beast halted its big head, and, throwing its great horns right back, sniffed the air. Its eyes seemed turned towards our hiding-place. But there were others behind who were impatient to get out, and a native woman darted forward, and beat the beast's buttocks with a hoe. The boy on his back, unconscious of the danger in front, drummed his little heels on the black, hairless sides, and the animal moved slowly and reluctantly forward.

One, two, three of the beasts stepped out; a fourth was already in the doorway, when suddenly came the shrill order from the whistle.

In an instant we were up and racing like madmen for the causeway, almost before the natives with their cattle had realised what had happened.

Lipthay was in front, leading me by 6 feet; we had been lying nearest to the path. Tho was panting along at my side. My Hungarian chum was now on the dyke, but he slipped on the wet clay, and came down with a crash. Both of us jumped clear of him, and went sliding along for several paces on the slippery surface. Soon we were up to the first buffalo, which was trying to turn. Tho leaned forward, and drove his bayonet into its hind quarters. With a roar it leaped off the path, and fell with a mighty splash into the pond, the boy still clinging to its back. I heard a peal of laughter somewhere behind me. On we went again, and the next instant were at the door, in which two of the beasts were wedged. Again the Doy's steel darted out, and one of the animals, with a bellow of pain, was forced through, like a cork pushed into a bottle.

In our ears rang the yells of the natives, beseeching each other to close the way.

The next instant we were through, and I saw a native heroically striving to pull away a bamboo pole, so as to let fall an inner gate; but before he could do so the rearmost buffalo, which was lumbering along in headlong flight, cannoned against him, and he was knocked sprawling. Tho had slipped in front, for we were now running in a narrow lane, where only one could pass at a time. The sides were walls of thick, sun-dried clay, in which, at irregular intervals, were little round loopholes. No one fired from them, though a few seconds had passed since the first alarm was given.

Behind us came the clatter of nailed boots, and I turned to see that Lipthay, his khaki and accoutrements caked with mud, had caught up with us. He laughed and puffed as my eye caught his. Every few yards the narrow way twisted and turned. We saw nothing, but could hear the cries of alarm of the natives and the thumping gallop of the terrified buffaloes just ahead. Suddenly the Doy turned off to the left, through a door in the wall, and the next instant we were in a kind of courtyard, covered with red tiles. In the middle was a guava tree in full bloom, and facing us a thatch-covered native house, with green blinds of split bamboo hanging from the roof.

As we advanced one of these was lifted, and a tall, lank native, holding a Winchester at the "ready," confronted us. His hair was long, and hung over his shoulders; his eyes, still full of sleep, had a fierce, wild glare in them.

We spread out and advanced towards him.

"The lu-thuong! (headman). Opium drunk," said Tho. "Surrender to us!"

The native spat at him, jerked up his weapon, fired at the Doy, and missed him.

Already he had pulled back the lever, preparing to shoot again, when Lipthay's rifle spoke. His weapon fell with a clang to the tiles, and, his two hands clasped to his breast, he staggered back against the screen, which gave way, and fell doubled up under the verandah. With his back against the wall of the house, he watched us as we came to the door. His mouth opened, and he tried to curse:

"De-oh!... de-oh!" Then he coughed, and a rush of blood choked his words. He toppled over on his side as our three rifle-butts, descending on its surface, splintered the wooden door of his abode. He had done his best to defend his guest.

The scene inside was a strange one. We had expected resistance, but found none, and were perhaps disappointed in consequence.

On a big wooden couch, and inside a green mosquito-curtain, lay a man, dressed in cream-coloured silk. Beside him was a tray on which I saw the little silver box, the skewers and the lamp. The latter was burning, and the brilliant stream of sunshine pouring through the broken door seemed to drown its flicker.

The man's face was long and emaciated, and, as the light struck it, I noticed that his skin was very fair for a native, that he wore a green silk turban, and that his hair was carefully rolled. The finger-nails of his left hand, which held the pipe over the flame, were very long; that of the little finger being at least 4 inches.

On the index finger of the same hand was a massive gold ring.

Beside him lay a woman, who was tending the opium, even as I had seen Ba do a few hours earlier. She was dressed in a long stole-like garment of bright green.

Neither of the pair moved or looked towards us, and for a few seconds their indifference to our presence seemed complete and contemptuous. When he had finished the pipe he had been smoking, he sat up and nodded to Tho, who saluted him in the vernacular, saying as he did so:

"Linh-binh, you must surrender and come with us. Fools, but not grave men, resist the inevitable."

There was a tremor in his voice, and a gleam in the little sergeant's eye that said only too plainly how gladly he would have slain the rebel then and there.

I noticed a glitter on the floor near the bed, bent down and picked up a Spencer carbine and a belt full of cartridges. Attached to it was a hunting-knife in a leather sheath, and a holster containing a revolver of an American pattern.

The linh-binh slid off the couch and stood before us.

"Cannot I die now?" he said to Tho.

"No! no! we are to take you alive. Such are the orders which must be obeyed." Then to me: "Camarade, you who are as strong as an ox, will you hold his arms behind his back one little moment?"

I did as he requested, and the Doy took the green turban from the head of our prisoner, and tied his elbows together, leaving about a yard of the silk loose, the end of which he wound round his own wrist.

Then we left the hut with our captive. As we passed under the verandah I saw that the lu-thuong was lying on his side, and seemed to be sleeping peacefully. He was quite dead. Lipthay picked up the Winchester, and walked with me behind Tho, before whom was the prisoner. We noticed that they were talking together in quite a friendly manner. The woman was following us, and I could hear the low sobbing complaint which she kept up as she trotted behind. We could hear much shouting, and the explosion of firearms in the village not far from us, and it was evident that the rebels were offering a stubborn but tardy resistance.

Guessing the importance of our capture, and fearing a rescue, both Lipthay and myself shouted to Tho to hurry on, and we all started off at a trot.

Outside, we found the Captain attended by a bugler. Our commanding officer was seated on a mound watching the gateway, and smoking his cigar. When we got up to him, he said:

"What have we here?"

"A rebel, mon capitaine," answered Lipthay.

"The linh-binh, mon capitaine," I replied.

"Linh-Nghi, mon capitaine," added Tho, who had learnt the name of the prisoner.

"And two rifles, and a pretty girl," added the officer with a laugh. Then he continued: "Leave all here in charge of Calvet (the bugler). You, Doy, go back to your section. You two men rejoin Sergeant Bevan in the village, and tell him to get his detachment together and rejoin me here."

When we reached the sergeant, all resistance had terminated, and the men were foraging in the huts or securing the prisoners.

We communicated the orders.

The little column assembled outside again, and we learned that two of our men had been slightly wounded; we had captured six prisoners, taken nine rifles, and five of the enemy had been killed. The surprise had been complete. Although few, if any, of us realised the importance of the capture we had made, it will presently be seen that our morning's work produced results which eventually aided not a little towards the success of the operations on a large scale undertaken against the rebels at the beginning of the following year. We reached Nha-Nam at eleven that morning, and an extra ration of wine was served out to us, as a compensation for the drenching we had received.

Our prisoners were lodged under the verandah of the house occupied by the native troops, where there was a barre de justice—heavy ironwood stocks—in which the right leg of each of the captives was secured. A guard, furnishing two sentries, was placed over them. They were well fed, and suffered no cruelty or insult; but, having been captured in armed rebellion, there existed no doubt as to what their ultimate fate would be.

It is now necessary to give some details concerning the important changes which were taking place at this time in the administration of the country.

The Government in Paris, influenced, no doubt by the growth of rebellion and rapine in the colony, had decided upon the appointment of a Governor-General armed with greater power than his predecessors.

For this purpose a decree, dated 20th April, 1891, was issued by the French Cabinet, which accorded that functionary great freedom of action. According to the new order of things, the Governor was vested with absolute power in the colony, and both the civil and military authorities therein were entirely under his control. All appeals or reports made by the heads of departments in Indo-China to the Minister in the metropolis were to pass through his hands.

At this time M. Picquet, the Governor, was just returning to France, and the Ministry appointed M. de Lanessan, a Radical deputy, who had already given proofs of superior ability in Parliamentary circles, and who was acknowledged to be a man possessing great initiative energy and activity.

The new Governor-General arrived in the East in May; and although his enemies have reproached him—and not without some cause—with want of tact and conciliation towards the military authorities, there can be no doubt that from his administration dates the era of commercial progress, which still continues in Indo-China.

He was the first to insist on the necessity of constructing railways and good roads in the colony, and, much as he did in this respect—for the first railway to Lang-son owes its origin to him—he would undoubtedly have done more had he not been hampered by the restricted finances at his disposal.

As it was, by his vehement insistence on the subject, he caused the investing public of France to realise the latent wealth existing in Tonquin, for the development of which it was absolutely necessary to construct good means of communication. He thus paved the way for his successors, MM. Rousseau and Doumer, who, thanks to his propaganda, eventually secured large loans, guaranteed by the Government, enabling them to construct a system of railways now almost terminated, traversing the whole of France's Eastern Empire, and penetrating into two of China's wealthiest provinces, Kwang-si and Yunan.

The first care of M. de Lanessan was to put an end to the intrigues existing at the court of Hué, having for their object the dethronement of the young king Than-Thai, and the restoration of the exiled Ham-Nghi to power. Also he took urgent measures to restore order in Tonquin.

To obtain these results he enquired into the grievances of the natives, and adopted pacific methods when possible; but when these were of no avail, he did not hesitate to employ rigorous and repressive measures. He undoubtedly possessed the necessary qualities for an administrator and organiser; and a few months after his arrival the Residents and local mandarins vied with each other in stamping out, with the aid of the native militia, the seeds of revolt and discord sown in the Delta, so that he was able to turn his attention to the central, northern and eastern districts of the colony, where rebellion and piracy existed in an armed and rampant state.

To ensure success in this work of pacification, M. de Lanessan made every effort to do away with the rivalry among the regular troops and the native militia, the latter being controlled by the civil Residents. To obtain this result he created in the unsettled provinces military zones—districts wholly administered by officers in the army—so that the powers and responsibilities of the different authorities were clearly divided and defined. The all-powerful military authorities were alone responsible for all that went on in the region committed to their care, and to the civil authorities was entrusted the administration of the Delta provinces.

This system proved such an excellent one that it has been maintained to this day, with few modifications; and at the beginning of 1903 there were, in Tonquin, four military zones divided up into nine districts, with a total population of about 2,000,000, and a superficial area of 20,000 square miles.

Thanks to the system introduced by M. de Lanessan, organised rebellion no longer exists in the colony, and, although the provinces bordering on Kwang-si and Kwang-tung are occasionally ravaged by the Chinese bands which cross the frontier, the pacification of the country may be said to be complete.

That the commercial progress of the colony was a slow one at this period there can be no doubt, but it was owing principally to the want of means of communication with the interior, and also to the prohibitive customs tariff and exorbitant transit rates on goods passing through to China, which had been adopted by the French Government.

To-day things have considerably improved, thanks to the railways already built, and they will go on improving when all the lines are completed. But unless the authorities adopt a broader policy with regard to transit duties on foreign goods imported into Yunan through Tonquin, reduce the railway freights and modify the existing scale of duties, the realisation of the full value of the country as a speedy and safe route to the central Chinese markets, with the consequent prosperity which would result, will be lost to

France; and private enterprise, which as yet has developed but slowly, notwithstanding the undisputed agricultural and mineral wealth of the Tonquin, will be brought to a standstill.

CHAPTER V

The five prisoners captured with Linh-Nghi were executed the first week in August. They had been tried and condemned by the native mandarins entrusted with the administration of justice. These functionaries had come over on purpose from Bac-Ninh in great state, and the execution took place in an open space in front of our fort. We supplied a guard and picquet for the occasion.

None of the rebels had given any information, although it was whispered that the native judges had submitted them to torture during their interrogation. We had no means of controlling these rumours, for each morning the prisoners were handed over to the native police, and they were returned at night; and, although they slept in the fort, it was forbidden to communicate with them. From their appearance and evident exhaustion I should be inclined to think they had suffered maltreatment. There would be nothing very surprising in this, for according to the native code of justice such methods were not only recommended, but were actually indicated. It is certain that the rebels showed no mercy to the loyal natives or French soldiers they captured alive (fortunately it was rarely, indeed, that any of the latter fell into their hands), and subsequently it was destined that I should witness shocking proofs of the terrible cruelty they were capable of employing.

It is therefore probable that the native judges made use of all the powers afforded them by the law of the land, and did not employ European methods—for which, most likely, they possessed supreme contempt.

The execution was carried out in a very simple and expeditious manner.

When a rectangular space had been cleared and lined by the troops, the two mandarins, dressed in robes of embroidered silk, of which the dominant colours were red and gold, their long hair neatly rolled in a new crepon turban, took up a position in the middle of one side of the square, and facing the centre.

Behind them were massed their retainers. Bannermen carried tattered triangular flags, and coolies bore aloft enormous umbrellas—two to each official—whereon were painted in bright colours a quaint design of dragons and griffins. Each mandarin was also accompanied by a sword-bearer, a pipe-bearer, and a domestic to whose care was confided a black-lacquered box containing the areca-nut and betel-leaf of his master. They formed a dirty, motley crowd, without order or cohesion—clad in shabby, tattered scarlet uniforms; and they laughed, chatted or squabbled, one with the other, like a pack of old fishwives.

They subsided into comparative silence, however, on the appearance of Captain Plessier, our commander, who occupied the place of honour, a little in advance of the two judges.

The prisoners were now brought into the enclosure, under the escort of a few linh-le (soldiers of the mandarin guard), whose dirty green uniforms and still dirtier rifles and accoutrements were certain proofs of their slovenly and undisciplined habits.

Behind the little procession formed by the condemned men stalked the executioner, a tall native dressed in a red embroidered vest and black silk pantaloons. Upon his shoulder he carried a heavy curved sword, about 3 feet long, and a good deal broader at the end than near the handle.

The five rebels, their hands tied behind them, walked to their death without any tremor or hesitation. Chatting together merrily, they threw curious glances at their surroundings, and expectorated from time to time, with evident unconcern, the red juice of the betel-leaf they were chewing.

They were lined up, separated about four paces one from the other, on the opposite side of the square occupied by the authorities, and facing them.

As each of the prisoners reached the place assigned to him, a native soldier unbuttoned and turned back the collar of the rebel's vest; then, one after the other, they knelt upon the grass, taking every care that their position should be as comfortable as the circumstances would allow.

The sentence having been read aloud to the assembled natives, the executioner, after thrusting his finger into his mouth, traced a wet line of red betel juice across the back of the neck of the first of his victims, about half an inch above the last big vertebra. Stepping back a pace, he swung aloft his heavy sword with both hands. It poised a second in the air; there was a glitter in the bright sunlight as it descended; then a swishing sound and a dull thud. The head of the first rebel, detached with a single blow, fell on the ground and rolled once over.

From the severed neck a rich red stream shot out quite 6 feet over the grass; the body rocked once and subsided gently. Bending over it, the executioner touched the open arteries, and smeared a little of the warm blood over his own lips as a charm against any evil influence from the spirit of the departed.

The other prisoners, who had watched the execution of their comrade with evident interest, made flattering remarks concerning the skill of the swordsman.

The next to die smiled, and prepared himself calmly, stretching his neck as far forward as it was possible for him to do without losing his balance.

I felt deadly sick, and could not bring myself to watch the succeeding decapitations, which were carried out with similar skill and expedition.

The bodies of the condemned were handed over to their families, but their heads, attached to the top of a tall bamboo pole, were exposed at the entrance of the fort as an example to all rebels.

The authorities had decided not to hurry on the trial of Linh-Nghi, in the hope that they would eventually succeed in obtaining information from him. He was interrogated during several days by the two mandarins, who failed, however, to extract the slightest indication of the strength of the enemy or the whereabouts of their positions. After the departure of these functionaries, our commander made several attempts, with the aid of Tho as an interpreter, to break through the reserve of the chieftain, but without success.

The treatment accorded him was a humane one; his diet was unstinted, and his parents, an aged, white-haired couple, were allowed to visit him as often as they chose during the daytime. His wife—for so the woman whom we had found with him proved to be—remained constantly by him, and attended to all his wants.

To one privation only was he submitted, and that was the want of opium. On this point our Captain was obdurate, and though Linh-Nghi, who was well supplied with money, offered to purchase the drug, his craving was not allowed satisfaction. To all his entreaties the same reply was given: "Speak! tell us what we ask of you, and you shall have opium—the very best—at our expense."

Only those who have witnessed the powerful hold the subtle drug takes on its votaries can imagine the torture endured by this native during the hours at which he had accustomed himself to indulge in his passion. These agonies, occurring shortly after the noon and evening meals, would commence by protracted yawnings, and develop into spasmodic, nervous contractions of the body and limbs, which broke into profuse perspiration. Unable to stand the strain, the unhappy victim of the brilliant-hued, but treacherous flower, or rather its seed, would entreat his guards to supply him with the smallest particle at no matter what price; then, finding that his supplications were without avail, he would break into a torrent of invective and malediction, which grew in intensity and filthiness as his increasing and impotent rage neared its climax. Then, speechless and foaming at the mouth, he would fall back on the hard, beaten-clay floor of the verandah, with mouth agape and black eyes fixed, staring at the roof above; his face, pale yellow, framed in the thick, tangled mass of long black hair escaped from his fallen turban. His chest would heave and crack under the short, sharp pants which brought the air through the larynx with a whistling hiss. Thus would he continue for perhaps an hour, until, exhausted by the struggle, he would fall into a sound sleep, from which he would awake refreshed and smiling, to laugh and chat with his guards, his wife or parents, if they happened to be present. Had there been any real danger to Linh-Nghi during these attacks I believe that opium, or some anæsthetic, would have been administered to him by our surgeon, M. Joly, who, on several occasions, was present during these crises.

On the 22nd August our prisoner made a daring bid for liberty. During the night he had succeeded in picking the lock which secured the two heavy beams forming the stocks wherein his ankles were imprisoned. At four in the morning, profiting by the fact that the native sentry was slumbering—though the soldier denied this, and attributed the chieftain's escape to the miraculous—Linh-Nghi made a dash for the palisade, and was astride it, when a native sergeant, who had heard the rattling of the bamboo, ran to the spot from whence the sound came, and succeeded in grasping a leg of the escaping rebel, to which he clung, shouting the while for help. A few seconds later the prisoner was brought back and secured, and the doctor attended to his wounds, for he had been almost impaled during his struggle by the pointed bamboo poles of the palisade.

Shortly after this incident a terrible tragedy occurred, which brought about a complete change in the attitude of our prisoner, and eventually made him a devoted partisan of the French cause.

Linh-Nghi had enemies in the rebel camp, and one of these, desirous of taking over his honours and command, informed De-Nam that the captive linh-binh had succumbed to pressure, and had given information to the French. He also provided evidence, which was false, to substantiate his declaration. Enraged at the apparent weakness of one of his most trusted lieutenants, the rebel chief decided to make an example, and he gave orders for the immediate seizure and execution of Linh-Nghi's aged parents. The details of this drama, which I obtained from Tho, were confirmed by documents captured later from the rebels. I had an opportunity of perusing them whilst serving on the staff of the 1st Brigade some months later.

At daylight on the morning of the 28th August, the European sentry at the gate of Nha-Nam found a basket, which had been deposited outside during the night. On being opened it was found to contain two heads and a letter addressed to our prisoner.

It is unnecessary to give further explanations, or to describe in morbid details the reception of this strange parcel by the unfortunate Linh-Nghi.

Certain it is that its effect was immediate, for that very evening I saw our ci-devant rebel, who had just returned from a long interview with our commander, under the verandah, his former prison, where he was squatting side by side with Tho, with whom he was engaged in a most friendly conversation; whilst, with some damp clay and split bamboo, he was constructing, with nimble fingers, neat little models of the different fortified positions belonging to his chief of yesterday.

From that time forward he was allowed all the opium he cared to smoke, and, though for his own safety he preferred to remain in the fort during several weeks, he was liberated, and lodgings were assigned to his wife in the native soldiers' village. Linh-Nghi now became a scout and guide to the French columns, and as such he rendered immense services to the authorities, concerning which more will be mentioned hereafter. Eventually, he was made a mandarin, and is now a local prefect of a district formerly overrun by rebellion. He and Tho became fast friends, and from their evening talks, when the "black smoke" hung thick under the thatch, I was able to derive much amusement and some knowledge.

Owing to information furnished by Nghi, the authorities decided to reconnoitre a road which had not been visited by French troops since 1886, when a column, under Major Dugenne, went by it from Tin-Dao (the old name for Nha-Nam), to Thaï-Nguyen, an important town situated on the Song-Cau river, about 20 miles as the crow flies to the north-west of Nha-Nam. This road had probably been constructed several centuries before, but, owing to the depopulation of the districts through which it passed, and also to its proximity to the forest-covered, mountainous region to the south, it was now but a path, which in some places completely disappeared in the ever-advancing jungle.

From a military point of view the reconnaissance of this route was of the greatest importance, since, should it be found practicable to infantry, it would be possible to make use of it, when the time served, as the means of advance for a column destined to attack the enemy's positions on the right flank.

In Thaï-Nguyen there was a garrison consisting of two companies of the Foreign Legion, one of native infantry, a section of mountain artillery, and a detachment of militia.

My squad formed part of the small column which left Nha-Nam on the 4th September, at five in the morning, to explore this road.

Though it had been supposed that the distance to be covered would not exceed 25 miles, we actually marched close upon 35 before reaching our destination.

At intervals we were obliged to cut our way through the vegetation which had invaded the track, and it was only by using the utmost care that our little party succeeded in keeping in the right direction.

On several occasions we disturbed big herds of deer, which scampered away on our approaching them; the tracks of tigers were frequently visible, and once the advance guard, consisting of half a dozen tirailleurs, were considerably startled by the presence of a fine python which lay basking in the sun, close by the track. It was only after several stones had been thrown at it that the big snake decided on withdrawing into the long grass. Owing to the advisability of concealing our movements from the enemy, it was deemed necessary not to make use of firearms on this occasion.

The men suffered much owing to the extreme heat; the path was in the worst of conditions, and we were obliged to twice ford a river, which, though not very deep, was exceedingly rapid, so that our expedition proved to be a very arduous one to all who took part in it.

It was nearly 8 p.m., and quite dark, when we reached our destination, and several of the men fell exhausted whilst waiting in the ranks for a hut to be prepared for us to pass the night in. Thaï-Nguyen possessed a fine citadel, of the Vauban style, which was built in 1798, and it was in this that the garrison dwelt.

The town and its neighbourhood was at this time infested by tigers, which prowled about the streets after dark, so that it was imprudent for the inhabitants to go out without a torch or a light of some kind. So great was the voracity and daring of these animals that on several occasions they had penetrated into the citadel and carried off dogs and goats belonging to the garrison. Indeed, the doctor, by an extraordinary stroke of good luck, killed one with a revolver shot as it was groping under his bed in search of a favourite pointer which had taken refuge there. Report had it that the lucky slayer of this greedy feline was so excited by his good fortune that he was found more dead than alive by the guard who ran to the hut on hearing the report of his weapon.

He lost his dog, however, for the poor animal was found to be quite dead, its skull crushed beneath the powerful paw of its enemy.

Our column, having proved that the road explored could, if necessary, serve as a means of penetration into the enemy's country, left Thaï-Nguyen on its return journey the next day at 4 p.m.

Lipthay had been in charge of the topographical work during our exploration, and his sketch of the route so pleased Major Berard, who commanded our battalion and was also in charge of the military zone, that my chum was detained in Thaï-Nguyen, and attached to the staff there. I was very sorry to lose him, but, for his sake, was glad of this change in his prospects, as his new position brought with it a greater chance of promotion.

Our party did not return to Nha-Nam by the same route it had come, but took a better known and more frequented track, passing more to the south, through a district more populated, and consequently better cultivated.

On our way back we slept one night at Cassong-Thuong, a small fort garrisoned by a detachment of militia under the orders of a European officer. We continued our journey the following morning, and reached Nha-Nam at 6 p.m.

Owing to the fact that the military authorities were now in possession of reliable information concerning the rebel's strength and positions, orders were issued by the Brigade for reconnaissances to be made from time to time, into the districts north of our fort, with a view to exploring the region and obtaining topographical sketches of the country, to be used in the production of a reliable map, for the use of the officers who were to assist in the big column, which the Government had decided to put in the field during the winter months. I took part in the first of these little expeditions on the 12th September, the object of which was to determine whether the track to Long-Thuong, a rebel village which had not been visited since January, was still accessible to infantry, and also to see if the hamlet was inhabited and fortified. We started out from Nha-Nam at three in the afternoon. As it was not intended to make any attack on the enemy should they be in force, our detachment was a weak one, composed only of thirty Legionaries and as many tirailleurs. In order to make things easy for the Europeans, for the heat was very oppressive, we were instructed to take with us only the six packets of ammunition contained in our belt-pouches—36 rounds. Fortunately for us all the tirailleurs, who accompanied us, started with 120 rounds per man.

We arrived within a quarter of a mile of our destination, which was about a league and a half to the north of our position, without incident.

The fields were well cultivated, and the rice was being harvested, but on our approach, the reapers—all women—fled with loud cries towards the hamlet. It is probable that the suspicions of Captain Plessier were aroused, for, by his orders, we left the path, extended and advanced towards the village across the cultivated ground; a small reserve remaining upon the track under the orders of Lieutenant Bennet.

When about 200 yards from the position, we were received by a hot fire from a strong party of the enemy occupying the hamlet. Our line halted, and took cover by kneeling behind the little embankments which separated one field from the other. From here we replied to the rebels, but, a few minutes later, were exposed to a severe cross-fire coming from the left flank; and, in less time than it takes to describe, a tirailleur was killed, and two others and one Legionary were wounded.

The enemy who took part in this flanking movement were some of De-Nam's regulars, who came from their entrenched positions in the forest, having been summoned to assist by their friends in the village, who for this pur-purpose made use of long, copper speaking-trumpets, the weird bellowings of which we could hear above the reports of the rifles and the repeated words of command.

Our reserve had extended on our left, at right angles to our line, but its fire failed to keep the enemy in check, and very soon we could distinguish their skirmishers, as they advanced in line at regular intervals, dropping now and again on one knee to discharge their rifles at us.

The situation was getting too warm to be pleasant, and most of the Legionaries having expended their slender stock of ammunition, it was found necessary to distribute among us the cartridges of the men who had been placed hors de combat, and also to take a few packets from each of the native infantrymen. Thanks to the wall-like ridges behind which we lay, we suffered no further casualties, but our cartridges were getting scarcer each minute, and we felt that should any of the enemy succeed in getting out of the village by an exit—which might possibly exist—other than the door before us, there would be a possibility of an attack on our right flank, and consequently a danger of the road to Nha-Nam being closed to us. It was very soon found necessary to restrict the efforts of the native troops to volley-firing, for, notwithstanding the repeated efforts of their French sergeants, they expended their ammunition with reckless extravagance when acting independently. The majority of them, not waiting to select a suitable target or to aim carefully, just loosed off into space, happy so long as the excitement created by the report of their rifle and the smell of their burning powder stayed their rising fears.

This was the first time I had seen our Captain under fire, and it was a supreme satisfaction to me to note that his attitude came up in every respect to the descriptions given me by my comrades, senior to myself in the service. Calm and collected, he had an eye for every detail, and seemed to foresee each new development in the situation. He was never a man of many words, and now he spoke only to give some short, crisp order to the bugler, or to a non-commissioned officer. Though he happened that day to be dressed in a suit of white drill, he was the only one among us who took no cover, and was in consequence the target for many a rebel rifle. As he walked coolly up and down behind the line of our crouching figures, his helmet cocked over his right ear, a cigarette between his lips, flicking his leggings every now and again with the cane he carried, he seemed to defy death itself. This attitude inspired his men with enthusiastic confidence, and every Legionary present would have hailed with joy an order from him to fix bayonets and charge right at the enemy.

The action had lasted but a few minutes when the order to retreat by echelons was given. The object of the reconnaissance had been accomplished, for it was clear that the track followed was accessible, and also that the village was occupied in force as an outpost; and under the circumstances it would have been a culpable breach of the art of war, a wanton invitation to disaster, to have continued the engagement.

Our retirement was not effected without some difficulty, for the enemy showed considerable daring and initiative in harassing our retreat; and our progress was slow, because we were embarrassed by our dead and wounded. Some difficulty was also experienced by the French sergeants in keeping their tirailleurs in hand, and it was undoubtedly due to their efforts, and also to the example of cool steadiness displayed by the Legionaries, that our withdrawal was saved from degenerating into a total sauve-qui-peut. It was found necessary to tell off men of my corps to bear away our comrades who were hors de combat, for the native troops were too plainly victims to shattered nerves to bear the strain of this task under fire. This somewhat reduced the strength of our little firing line, which, however, received some assistance from Lieutenant Bennet, who picked up a rifle and "downed" several of our eager pursuers, for he was a first-class marksman.

The enemy abandoned their attack when we were about a mile from Nha-Nam; but it was a band of tired and thirsty men that reached the shelter of our position that evening at seven.

Warned by our Captain, who had galloped on ahead of us as soon as all danger had ceased, the guard turned out and rendered the usual honours to the dead and wounded as they were borne through the gate of the fort.

The wounded were at once attended to in the infirmary, and were transferred under escort the next morning to the hospital at Phulang-Thuong.

On the day following our engagement the whole garrison turned out under arms to assist at the funeral of the tirailleur who had been killed. He was buried in the small, well-kept cemetery, situated just below the slope to the north-west of our position. The French people have had at all times a great respect for their dead, and their soldiers whose lot it has been to lay down their life, au champ d'honneur, as they so eloquently express it, have always received their full share of the respect paid to the departed. In France there exists a fund, known as L'Œuvre des tombes, subscribed to by thousands of the charitable public; and the money thus obtained is expended on the hundreds of far-away colonial graveyards, which are kept in excellent order, and in erecting an iron cross, bearing the name and corps of the deceased, over the last resting-place of each soldier of the Republic who falls in fight or dies of disease. This is done without restriction of race or religion.

I went to see Tho that evening, and found Linh-Nghi with him. They both amused me by their evident regret at not having assisted in the engagement of the previous day.

The little sergeant's complaints were based on plain, unsatisfied bloodthirstiness; those of my ex-rebel friend clearly originated in that spirit of unslakable vengeance which only an Asiatic can acquire. It was instructive to note how they, after each pipe of opium, built fresh plans, and devised new methods for the merciless slaughter of their enemies. From them I learnt that a spy had come in during the day with information that De-Tam, the most capable of all the rebel military leaders, had been in command of the troops that had attacked us; and that this famous captain, for whom they evidently cherished much hate, and a good deal of reluctant admiration, had been severely wounded towards the end of the fight, his left arm having been shattered by a bullet just below the shoulder. This proved to be a fact.

I met the famous chieftain in 1897, when he was a partisan of the French, and the crippled state of his limb—due, no doubt, to the elementary treatment of the wound by the native medicine-man—was an evident proof of it.

I passed many pleasant evenings with Tho and Nghi, who would favour me with stories of war and love, legends of ancient origin, in which the actors were demi-gods, dragons and genii, and strange fables full of local colour, replete with quaint proverbs and philosophical axioms dear to the disciples of Confucius. Unfortunately, I was soon to be deprived of the real pleasure obtained from these foregatherings, for my section received orders to proceed to Cho-Trang, and I was thus suddenly separated from my two friends. It was not without some regret that I accepted this hazard of a soldier's life, against which one should not murmur; and I was really sorry that the opportunity afforded me for the study of the complex characteristics of Tho and Nghi should have been such a brief one.

My new location was a small fort situated to the north-west, on the confines of the Yen-Thé province, about 60 miles from Nha-Nam as the crow flies, but a good 80 by road. Owing to its position in a rugged, forest-clad mountainous region, and to its being surrounded, a few hundred yards away, by a chain of rocky heights, green with the vegetation which flourished in the crevices, it was found to be so unhealthy that the military authorities had, up till October 1891, contented themselves with maintaining a garrison of native soldiers there. Owing, however, to the approaching operations against the rebels, and to the fact that Cho-Trang was situated on the left flank of their positions, and close to several paths leading into their country, it was found necessary to strengthen the force there for a few months; since by these tracks it would be quite possible for some of the Chinese bands, established in the hills around Lang-son, to come to the assistance of De-Nam.

From Nha-Nam our detachment marched via Cao-Thuong to Phulang-Thuong, whence we served as an escort to a convoy going to Lang-son. We went by the famous mandarin road which had been the scene of the retreat of General de Négriers army in March, 1885.

Our rate of progress was a slow one, for the vehicles we escorted were heavy carts, drawn by tame buffaloes, or native wheel-barrows of a most peculiar pattern, constructed entirely of bamboo and ironwood, without a single nail or screw. The wheel consisted of a big wooden disc about 3 feet in diameter, which revolved on a teak axle, and produced a loud scratching noise as these clumsy carriages trundled over the rough road. The regulation load for these barrows was about 180 pounds, and to each of them there were two Chinese coolies. One pushed the barrow from behind, with a strap, each end of which was attached to a handle, passing over his shoulders, and thus relieving the wheel of some of the weight carried; and another was in front, hitched to a rope tied to the horn of this prehistoric little vehicle. The creaking of the wheels and continued yelling chatter of the Chinese created a perfect pandemonium of sound. Our convoy was more than 2 miles long, so that when the head had reached a halting-place, and its escort was able to obtain rest and refreshment, the unfortunate soldiers in the rear were still toiling slowly along, and would arrive at an étape to find that only a short space of time remained for them to refresh their tired legs and empty stomachs.

After Kep, the scene of Major Dugenne's reverse in June, 1884, the road passed through a stretch of scenery wild and magnificent. By a succession of loops and curves the route rose and passed round the flank of one mountain after another. Sometimes the convoy crept slowly over small bridges spanning mountain torrents, overhung with dense, tropical vegetation. Now the road would wind through beautiful thickets of bamboo, so dense that it would have been impossible to penetrate it. At times we skirted deep woods and charming combes full of thick undergrowth, palms and creepers. Often the track dipped and traversed fine valleys, covered with waving jungle grass; beyond this could be seen a vista of hills overrun with black forest, or chain upon chain of massive rocks, 1,000 feet high, all bedecked with variegated foliage. On or near the track there were few signs of animal or bird life, with the exception of the ubiquitous sparrow and the ever-present kite, though the vanguard occasionally disturbed a flight of chattering parrakeets, or scared away small herds of deer, which, with a few bounds, would disappear into the jungle. We halted at Kep, Sui-ganh and Bac-Lé, and passed the night in the forts at these places. Here the convoy was packed in an enclosure surrounded by a high bamboo fence, fires being kept burning all night to scare away tigers and panthers, as there were many in the jungle along the road.

The coolies, on their arrival, were told off into squads, and the daily ration of rice and salt fish was served out to them. This they cooked in copper pots, and the men of each squad squatted round the fires awaiting their evening meal, while one of their comrades, who acted as cook for the occasion, kept stirring the stew with a bamboo stick.

Most of these Celestials were tall, well-made men, whose lower limbs were abnormally developed—a natural result of the calling they followed—and, like the majority of their race, they evidently possessed a strong dislike to soap and water, for they were extremely filthy. They were clothed, like the men of the mountain tribes in this region of the Tonquin, in a costume consisting of a vest and pantaloons of blue cotton cloth, which, in most cases, was in a terribly ragged condition.

For pay they received twenty-five cents per diem (about fivepence), plus their daily rations.

The meal finished, the majority indulged in a few pipes of cheap opium, locally known as Sai, and the surface of the compound was starred over with the numerous tiny twinkles of their little lamps. These went out one by one, and before midnight the camp was plunged in silence and slumber, the naked limbs of the sleeping coolies having the appearance of old ivory or new bronze in the flickering glimmer of the watch-fires, round which they reclined. Then the stillness of the night would be broken only by the song of the cicalas, the crackle of burning wood, the occasional call of the sentries, and the far-away cop! cop! cop! of a tiger hunting in the hills.

At Bac-Lé our detachment left the convoy, and abandoning the highroad, we struck off due north by a small path which led to Cho-Trang. We set out before daybreak, so as to avoid marching in the midday heat, and were accompanied by a guide and several coolies bearing lighted torches made of split bamboo as a precaution against wild beasts.

Cho-Trang is about 12 miles from the Lang-son road, and the little track we followed passed for nine of these through a succession of jungle-covered valleys, and over hills hidden in primeval forests of teak, banyan, ironwood and palm trees, some of which were of enormous size, with an impenetrable undergrowth of fern, interlacing creepers, orchids and spiked rattan. In these woods the light of day was almost shut out by the dense foliage; no birds seemed to live there, and the strange, weird silence was only broken now and again by troops of chattering brown monkeys, which, disturbed by our approach, would scuttle away through the branches, jumping from one bough to another with their usual agility, and maintaining the while such grotesqueness of face and demeanour that our laughter was frequently provoked.

When we had marched about five hours, for during the darkness the pace had been a slow one, we found ourselves close upon the rocky chain already described, which exactly resembled the pinnacles which rise in hundreds from the sea in Along Bay. This strange configuration is known as the Nui-dong-Nghi, and its jagged ridges run east from this point right through Tonquin into Kwang-si, and also far north to the heart of the province of Cao-Bang.

We traversed the first chain through a pass known as the Deo-Mou-Phieu, which in some places is so narrow that a native pony can only just squeeze between the projecting boulders. This narrow cleft is evidently the thousands-of-years-old work of the waters, which have eaten a way through the calcareous rock. Indeed, there rushed through the pass a rapid though narrow stream, wherein we had to wade knee-high.

Between these high stone walls the scenery possessed a savage grandeur I have never seen equalled, and the semi-darkness of the narrow way produced a most awesome effect. A few lines from La Mort de Rolland, recited by a comrade during one of the short halts we made, produced such a feeling of intense sadness that I was glad when our little column broke out of these weird surroundings into the bright sunshine beyond.

From the pass, which was nearly a mile long, we debouched into a little circular plain, with a superficial area of about 1½ square miles. It was surrounded by high rocky walls, to all appearance without a break in them, and the fort of Cho-Trang was situated almost exactly in the middle of the plain.

We found that the position was a solid one. It was rectangular in form, with a small bastion at each angle, and the fortification consisted of a well-built parapet and ditch, round which ran the usual bamboo palisades.

Our little detachment of thirty men was lodged in a big, one-roomed hut of clay and bamboo, thatched with macaw palm. It had evidently been prepared for our use, for it was clean and freshly whitewashed, and contained the necessary bedding and mosquito-nets for the detachment.

The fort was in command of a lieutenant of the tirailleurs Tonkinois an eccentric individual who had a strong aversion to the Legionaries. Not that he was unnecessarily harsh or unjust towards us, but he had a mania for openly expressing a want of confidence in our discipline, which wounded the pride of the men of our detachment, the majority of whom soon hated him most cordially. He was married, according to native custom, to a

Tonquinese woman, who was living in the fort; and this, added to the fact that he was an opium-smoker, did not aid in increasing the small respect with which he was regarded by the Legionaries.

Strict orders had been given by the General commanding the Brigade that we should not be overworked while staying in this unhealthy spot, so that our life was rather a quiet and monotonous one. The only exciting incident that happened during my stay here was an attack made on the cattle stockade by two black panthers. One of these beasts succeeded in gaining an entrance, and killed a bullock. He paid for his daring with his life, however, and was riddled with bullets by some Legionaries who had been awakened by the cries of the native sentry.

The nights were gradually becoming cooler, for we were now in the middle of October, and life was rendered unpleasant by the thick, damp mists which hung continually over our position. Owing to the high walls of rock surrounding the little plain upon which the fort was built, there was little or no breeze, so that these fogs hung about us till late in each morning, when the midday heat of the tropical sun dispelled them. No doubt this was one of the principal causes of the prevalence of fever in this district; another being that the water used by the troops, though it came from mountain streams, and was apparently limpid, was strongly impregnated with copper, of which metal there were considerable traces in the soil of the region. Filters were provided for the garrison, and the troops were not allowed to use any water, either for cooking or drinking, unless it had been previously boiled. Even these precautions did not suffice to avoid disease, for when our detachment had been three weeks in Cho-Trang, more than half of its effective was laid up with fever, which takes a most virulent form in this district.

Its commencement, like ordinary malaria, is generally announced by shivering fits, during which the sufferer experiences a sensation of extreme cold. The hands and feet are numbed and glacial; the teeth chatter continually, notwithstanding the fact that the thermometer in the verandah is often, in such cases, at 95 degrees. This is succeeded at the end of an hour or more by a feeling of burning heat; perspiration ceases, the sufferer's temperature rises to over a hundred; he is a victim of terrible pains in the head, and is often delirious. At Cho-Trang this condition was usually complicated by hematuric symptoms, which, fortunately, do not occur in the majority of cases of ordinary jungle fever.

There was no doctor in the fort (indeed, it would be impossible to maintain a medical officer in each of the numerous small garrisons in Tonquin), and it was the lieutenant who examined the sick men and served out the medicines provided by the authorities without stint.

In such cases commanders of forts are furnished with a manual, which is well written, and gives in the clearest of terms explanations concerning the symptoms and treatment of the different tropical and other diseases they will most probably be called upon to treat. Definite instructions are also given in this little book to the officers, concerning the transfer of the men to the nearest hospital centre, whenever there are signs that the disease from which they are suffering is of a persistent or malignant form. Though these recommendations are not always adhered to, it would hardly be fair in such cases to censure the commanders, since it often happens, on numerous removals of this kind being made, that the officer receives blame from headquarters for having neglected to take the necessary precautions to ensure the satisfactory sanitation of his post, whereas in most instances the epidemic has had its origin in the insanitary position of the fort, or the dangerous composition of the soil it was built on.

It was noticeable that the first among my comrades to fall victims to sickness were the younger members of the detachment. When they had a strong and healthy constitution they generally recovered, and though the fever clung to them for six months, and sometimes more, during which period the attacks gradually decreased in force and occurred at longer intervals, they eventually became seasoned, and the fever seemed no longer to have any hold on them. I know of a good many men who have served four consecutive years in the colony, and who, after paying a heavy toll to malaria, during the first year or eighteen months, have never again been troubled by the disease.

Hard drinkers were longer in resisting the attacks of the fever fiend, but once the illness got a hold upon them, the results were generally fatal. One of the peculiarities of the jungle fever, in any form, is that the sufferer loses all appetite; indeed, he usually exhibits almost a loathing for any kind of food. It is therefore necessary to maintain his vitality, which rapidly sinks under the repeated attacks of the disease. To obtain this result liberal allowances of liquid food are administered to the patient. In Tonquin, milk, either fresh or condensed, was the diet most frequently prescribed, and in most cases with excellent results, except when the sufferers happened to be confirmed alcoholic subjects. Then the patients would either refuse to take milk, for which they possessed a decided repugnance, or they would be unable to keep and digest it after having forced themselves to swallow it.

It is easy to understand that, owing to the number of men incapacitated through sickness, the duties of the few available for service were considerably increased. It was no unusual occurrence to find oneself detailed for guard three times in one week, and it was only by reducing things to their strictest limit that sufficient men could be found to escort the convoy which was brought from Bac-Lé every Thursday. The convoy was absolutely necessary, for we depended on this weekly service for our supply of food. A reserve stock of flour, wine, rice, coffee, sugar and salt, sufficient to feed the members of the garrison for three months, was stored in the fort; but this was only to be drawn upon in cases of extreme urgency, such as siege or blockade.

It was during this trying time that I was able to appreciate the good-fellowship and unobtrusive self-abnegation possessed by the majority of my comrades, and many instances of their kindly spirit came under my observation.

Whenever a man detailed for service fell sick shortly before going on duty—and this was by no means a rare occurrence—a chum would at once cheerfully volunteer and take his place, though, as often as not, he had himself just come off convoy or guard duty, or was recovering from an attack of fever.

The able men not on duty—they were generally but few—neglected their own comfort, and sacrificed their rare hours of rest to attend, without murmur, to their stricken comrades, and did their best, in their rough but kindly way, to lighten their sufferings.

It was a quaint and touching sight to watch one of these bearded mercenaries, as he passed from cot to cot, and note his efforts to repress his own impatience and clumsiness, as he piled blanket after blanket on a shivering sufferer, changed the damp linen of another, who had broken into the beneficent sweat that denoted the termination of an attack, or calmed, with a voice which he tried to render gentle, the ravings of a delirious friend, standing the while to change every few minutes the wet bandages on the burning brow of the stricken one.

With what gentle care the weak ones would be lifted into a sitting position, and how patiently, with cheery, though perhaps clumsy jokes, would these self-appointed nurses encourage their patients to drink the cup of milk which succoured the ebbing strength, or the boiling liquid that provoked the saving perspiration.

"Allons! mon vieux. You're not dead yet! The tree is not grown from which your pine overcoat will be made. Courage! take this, and to-morrow you will feel so well that you will want to go on convoy guard, so as to see that little brown congai that winked at you last time we were at Bac-Lé. Sly dog! Va!"

Or:

"Bien quoi! hold on, mon ami! There's a lot more wine in the storeroom that wants drinking. Don't desert us; we shall never get through it without the help of your steep throat."

Often I would laugh at their coarse wit, though a big lump in my throat betokened another kind of sentiment. Yet one might be joyful at the evidence of the vast store of human kindness possessed by these rough soldier-folk, which, though hidden till now, came splendidly to the fore in this time of common misfortune.

On the 20th November, as I was sitting on a stool close by the door of the fort—for I was feeling decidedly queer, having just recovered from a third severe attack of fever—the native sentry, who was posted on a little wooden platform about 20 feet high, supported on four bamboo poles, and fitted with a thatch roof, informed me with a shout that he could perceive a troop of European soldiers, accompanied by two mounted officers, coming out of the pass towards us. I was in charge of the guard for the day, so I sent off a tirailleur to inform the commander. A few minutes later the two officers seen by the sentry came galloping into Cho-Trang on their ponies, and my surprise was great on recognising Captain Plessier and Surgeon Joly.

As they came through the gate I rose and saluted. Our Captain drew up his little mount with a jerk, and after looking hard at me for a few seconds, exclaimed:

"Mon Dieu! Doctor, why, this is our Englishman. But how changed! Why, the man is as yellow as a buttercup, and as thin as a vine-pole."

While he was speaking, the doctor had dismounted, and, after throwing the reins to a native soldier who stood by, he came over to me. After consulting my pulse, and looking at my tongue, he turned to Captain Plessier and said:

"This man is in a high fever, and ought to be in bed."

He questioned me concerning the date on which I had had my first attack, and obliged me also to give him other details concerning my malady. Then he walked off and rejoined our Captain, who had gone on to the quarters of the lieutenant in command of the fort. A few minutes later a sergeant came up to the guard-house and told me that, on the doctor's advice, the lieutenant had given orders for me to be relieved, and he (the sergeant) had been instructed to tell me to go to bed.

I was not sorry for this, for I was feeling very unwell; and when one of my comrades put in an appearance I passed the service on to him, hurried away to my hut, and was soon lying on my cot under a pile of blankets, in anticipation of the attack of ague which was already giving me signs of speedy approach.

I had not been there long before Captain Plessier, accompanied by our surgeon, came into the room. They visited the sick men who were in their cots—there were nine besides myself—and then came over to me. After examining me again, the doctor said:

"This man should be sent down to the nearest hospital as soon as possible. He might leave with us to-morrow morning."

"We have not sufficient coolies to carry him," replied our Captain; "and it would take at least two days to get some from Bac-Lé." He reflected a little, and then asked me: "Can you ride?"

"Yes, mon capitaine," I answered.

"Well, doctor, I think the best thing will be to put him on my spare pony," continued our chief; "that is, if you think he can stand the ride, and one of our coolies can carry his baggage. Eh, doctor?"

"Yes, I think we can risk it, for it is better to get him away from here as soon as possible," answered M. Joly.

No sooner had our officers left the room than several of my comrades set to work to pack my kit, for I was now in a high fever again, and consequently too weak and ill to attend to this operation myself. As they bustled about, these good-hearted fellows, with many good-natured jokes concerning my coming journey to the "sea-side," congratulated me on my luck, and did their best to encourage me to get to sleep, so as to gain strength for my long ride on the morrow.

We started early the next morning, and though I was glad to leave the "Sale trou," as my comrades termed the fort, I was sorry at the thought that they would have to remain for several weeks longer in this unhealthy spot. Dr Joly had announced the previous evening to the other sick men that they would be removed as soon as sufficient coolies could be obtained for their transportation.

My mount was a big Tartar pony, whose only fault consisted in a persistent desire to leave the path and gallop through the forest. He succeeded in taking me unawares the first time, and my helmet was knocked off and I was nearly brained by the bough of a tree. Like most of these little horses, when they have been in the hands of the natives, he possessed a terribly hard mouth, so that what with this and the fever which had again taken a hold on me, I experienced a somewhat lively journey.

We reached Kep at four in the afternoon, and here I was put into a carriage on the little railway to Lang-son, which was then in course of construction, and had reached this point, 12 miles from Phulang-Thuong, a few days previously.

At Kep I said good-bye to my comrades who formed the escort, and thanked our Captain and doctor for their kindness. I afterwards learned that I had indeed reason to be grateful to them for my speedy transference, for a week elapsed before sufficient coolies could be obtained to transport the other sick men from Cho-Trang, and one of the poor fellows died during the journey.

On the arrival of the train at Phulang-Thuong a stretcher was in readiness for me, instructions to that effect having been telegraphed from Kep, and I was carried to the hospital. This establishment was virtually a sort of base ambulance, from which the patients, whom the doctors considered in need of a long treatment and change of climate, were sent on to Haïphong or Quang-Yen. It was, however, well built, possessed an efficient staff of surgeons and nurses, and was so fitted up that every colonial disease or casualty likely to occur during a campaign could be dealt with under the best of conditions. A great deal of money and attention is expended by the French Government in the building and fitting up of the hospitals in Tonquin, and the doctors are well trained, clever and conscientious men.

I remained here for a fortnight, during which time I do not think the fever left me for an hour; indeed, during the first six days I was almost continuously unconscious. I was treated with the utmost kindness and care, both by the surgeons and Sisters. These excellent women, who belong to the Roman Catholic Order of "St Vincent de Paul," do not, unfortunately, possess the same scientific knowledge of medical nursing as our British hospital nurses, but they are untiring in the care which they give to the patients, and their unstinted efforts to relieve the suffering are worthy of the highest praise.

During that period of my illness when the fever was at its worst and I was almost constantly delirious, it seemed to me that there were moments when some section of my intellect, escaping from the frenzy which possessed my brain, succeeded in retaining its lucidity, and was able to obtain control over a portion of my personality, inspiring it with a power to think and see independently of, and, as it were, apart from, the remainder of my suffering organism.

So vividly did this impression assert itself, that to this day I can remember hearing my own ravings, and mentally consoling myself with the thought that they were merely the results of delirium. I would at such times watch the terrifying hallucinations, conjured up by the malady, with a perfect knowledge that they were the results of an imagination distorted by the fever which possessed me; and at the same time find means to take notice of a tiny lizard, as it crawled, searching for mosquitoes, up the curtain surrounding my bed, the flickering night-light, the crucifix hanging on the whitewashed wall in front of me, or the Sister on duty as she moved silently from cot to cot, to administer medicine or to assure herself that her patients were asleep, and whose picturesque costume, white cornette and collar, reminded me of the poem, "The Black Musketeer," in the Ingoldsby Legends. My experience is by no means unique, for several of my friends who have also been victims to jungle fever, and with whom I have compared notes, have been impressed by phenomena of a similar description.

When my daily temperature began to take a slow but decidedly downward curve, the head doctor informed me that I was to be sent to the hospital at Quang-Yen, a small town situated on the coast not far from Along Bay, where, said he, aided by the sea-air, I might possibly succeed in shaking off the malaria; though he told me that he was noting my clinic-sheet to the effect that he considered it advisable to send me back to Algeria as soon as I could support the voyage. I felt much disappointed at this information, though I recognised his kindly intention; but it was far from my wish to return so soon to Africa, and I determined to make every effort, in the event of my getting rid of the fever, to induce the doctors at Quang-Yen to allow me to remain in Tonquin, for I still hoped to participate in the coming winter campaign in the Yen-Thé, the prospects of which had been a constant topic of conversation with my comrades. A few days later I was carried on board a river steamer, but during the journey I fell so ill again that I was put on shore at Haïphong, and remained three days in the hospital there. However, at the end of that period I was sufficiently recovered to continue my journey, and eventually reached Quang-Yen on the 12th November.

CHAPTER VI

The town of Quang-Yen, capital of the province of the same name, is situated about 10 miles to the south-east of Haïphong, and close to the sea. Thanks to its position on a series of small hills, it is swept by the sea-breeze, and enjoys a well-merited reputation for its healthy climate.

A fine hospital was erected here by the French in 1888; this has since been enlarged, and now affords accommodation for three hundred patients.

On my arrival I was placed in one of the big fever wards, each of which contained twenty-four beds, and the comfort and quiet of my new quarters, the skill and care of the doctors and Sisters, and the pure air of the region, soon produced most beneficial results.

The attacks of malaria decreased in frequency and intensity, and my strength augmented each day.

There was something delightfully fresh and reposeful in the sensation of finding oneself again in a comfortable bed, between spotless sheets; and the vista of the long room, with its polished wood floor, the neat cots of black-enamelled iron and shining brass, the white mosquito-curtains and the sound of the crackling log-fire, which burned in the open hearth during the early cool of the November mornings, reminded one of the cleanliness and ease of Europe—of home. It was pleasant, too, to watch the Sisters as they glided from bed to bed, attending with untiring patience and gentleness to the wants of the sufferers. It was both pathetic and droll to see one of these good women as, with the tender care of a mother, she washed the face and hands of some big and bearded Legionary who was too debilitated to do anything for himself, but who kept his eyes open, notwithstanding their smarting, so as not to lose a single movement of his ministering angel; continually expressing his thanks the while, at the risk of receiving a mouthful of soap and water. Neither could one watch without emotion a Sister who had to deal with a patient who had lost all desire for food, as was often the case with victims to persistent fever. Insisting on the sufferer partaking of a cup of beef-tea, she would administer it spoonful by spoonful, accompanying each of these with gentle words of encouragement, so that the rough mercenary could not do otherwise than gulp down the helpings—trying, meanwhile, to look pleasant and grateful. There was a little chapel attached to the hospital, wherein a Spanish missionary from a neighbouring village of Roman Catholic converts officiated; and when the men were convalescent and able to get about, they would manifest their gratitude to, and respect for, their nurses by attending mass on Sundays, notwithstanding the fact that many of them were Protestants, and that most of them possessed little or no religion at all under ordinary circumstances. The Sister who attended to me was a small and cheerful little person, who seemed to be about at all hours of the day and night, and her activity and ceaseless surveillance were the terror of the native servants who worked in the ward. She was a merry soul, who never missed an occasion for drawing a laugh from her patients. Should I hesitate and grimace before swallowing my dose of quinine—it was administered in solution in those days—she would assure me that to connaisseurs its taste was as agreeable as that of fin champagne, and declare that it was only a question of time and habit for me to be able to appreciate its delicate flavour.

I owe much to this Sister for the care and attention she gave me during my stay in Quang-Yen hospital—these were, of course, equally bestowed on all the sufferers under her charge—and it was my good fortune, five years later, to meet her under entirely different circumstances, when I recalled myself to her memory and expressed my gratitude. To-day, as I write, there comes back to me a vision of the ward at night, when, having fallen asleep after blinking at the reflection of the firelight on the polished parquet and brass knobs on the bedposts of the neighbouring cots, a gentle touch would awaken me from my first slumber, and I could see, under the white cornette, the smiling face of my nurse—en religion, Sœur Agnes—as, after lifting the mosquito-curtain, she presented to my lips a small glass containing the nightly dose of the bitter drug, while she whispered: "Tenez, mon petit St Jean—Voici votre grog."

After attending to the wants of each, and seeing that all are comfortable, Sœur Agnes would kneel down in the ward, and, with bent head and clasped hands, repeat in a soft but distinct voice the prayers for the night. Every soldier who was able to sit up in bed would do so, and nearly all those who could, murmured with her the Lord's Prayer, each in his own language. Probably most of them did so simply to please the patient religieuse, who soothed their sufferings and attended to their needs; but, be that as it may, there existed no regulation which obliged them so to do, therefore their action was spontaneous and impressive.

When the Sister had left the room, after bidding a general "good-night" to its occupants, it was very seldom that any conversation would take place. It seemed as if the majority of the men were anxious to court sleep while still under the impression left them by the saintly, self-sacrificing woman to whom they had just listened, desiring, perhaps, that it should bring to them dreams of those they loved, but of whom they never spoke. Now and again a new patient, proud of his cynicism, would scoff at his comrades, curse them for knock-kneed calotins, or go so far as to laugh aloud, or even whistle a ribald regimental ditty, during the evening prayer. They never did this twice, however, for a straight-spoken, though perhaps somewhat lurid, warning from their room-mates always sufficed to quell any desire for persistence in this breach of the etiquette of the ward. Had it been otherwise, it is certain that their suppression would have been both rapid and awesome.

On the 12th December I was called before the Repatriation Committee (Conseil de Rapatriement), the members of which—three doctors—seeing the progress I had made, decided to keep me in the hospital for another fortnight, at the end of which period, if no relapse had occurred, I could return to my corps. It is hardly necessary to state that this decision was very agreeable to me, for I had feared that these officers would order my return to Algeria; and once assured of the realisation of my desires, I improved rapidly in health and strength. Sometimes, when I suspected a slight attack of fever, I "faked" my temperature, lest the doctor who examined my "chart" each day should take another view of my case, and send me up again before the Committee. I trust, however, that this confession of my fault will bring with it forgiveness for the trick played upon my kind and trusting nurse.

During my stay at Quang-Yen I saw that the majority of the patients were men from the Infanterie de Marine. These regiments passed into the domain of the Minister of War in 1901, and are now known as L'Infanterie Coloniale. I was very surprised at their youthfulness and evident want of stamina. This corps was originally formed, like our Royal Marines, for service afloat. Since 1860 their place on board the men-of-war has been taken by sailors (fusiliers marins) who undergo a special course of training in musketry and infantry drill; and the Infanterie de Marine was formed into twelve regiments, which now garrison the naval ports on the French coast, the principal towns in the Colonies, and take part in all expeditions overseas. Before the reorganisation of the army, carried out after the Franco-German War, the men of this fine corps had won a grand reputation for courage and endurance, and the defence of the village of Bazeilles by a brigade of French marines against a division of Bavarian troops, in 1870, will ever remain one of the finest pages in the history of the struggle. General conscription and the short service system have done much to reduce the fighting value of these regiments, which were formerly composed of men who had been submitted to a most searching medical examination, and consequently stood a good chance of resisting the insalubrious climate of the Colonies, and who volunteered for a long period with the flag. To-day, the majority of these troops are town-bred, beardless boys, of from eighteen to twenty years of age, who are in these regiments because they have been unfortunate enough to draw a low number from the conscription-urn. Like all France's sons, they are brave and enthusiastic, but owing to their youth, inexperience and hurried and incomplete military training they have sometimes proved victims to sudden panic, and their but half-formed constitutions and still growing physique make them prompt sufferers to malady, fatigue and discouragement during the hardships of a tropical campaign. Several French authorities on military matters have expressed the opinion that the Government would do well to employ more seasoned material for their colonial garrisons and expeditions, and reserve these brave youths for the future battlefields of Europe, whereon may be decided the destiny of their fatherland.

Those of us who were able to get about attended the midnight mass on Christmas Eve, and the little chapel, with its interior prettily decorated by the willing efforts of the convalescent soldiers, was full to overflowing; and, though probably the thoughts of the majority present wandered away to the homeland, we joined vigorously in the joyful anthem, "Noel! Noel! Voici le Redempteur!" to the visible satisfaction of the beaming, buxom sœur supérieure and the smiling Sisters. On the 30th I found myself "Exeat"—i.e., discharged from the hospital as cured—on the deck of a little river steamer which was churning her way through the red, muddy waters of the Cua-Cam, past miles of mangrove swamp, towards Haïphong.

The weather was bright, dry and cold—a typical winter's day of this part of the world—and the pure, crisp air, reminding me of home, seemed delightfully invigorating after the stifling, damp heat of the past summer months. At Haïphong I boarded another boat, which landed me in Phulang-Thuong the next morning.

Here I found signs of the coming campaign, for several little river-steamers were discharging their cargoes of stores, ammunition and material, and hundreds of coolies were employed in transporting the goods to the big Government go-downs in the little town, where they were stored for the time being. From here large quantities of flour, tinned beef and other stores were forwarded to Nha-Nam and Bo-Ha, these forts in turn serving as bases, from which the different columns were revictualed. On my arrival, I reported at the office of the garrison major, expecting to receive orders to leave by the first opportunity for Nha-Nam, via Cao-Thuong—that is, by the same route which our detachment, just landed from the Bien-Hoa, had taken eight months previously—but information was given me by one of the military secretaries to the effect that I would have to wait a few days, pending the formation of a convoy which was to proceed in sampans, up the Song-Thuong river, to Bo-Ha, and that I would form one of the escort, to be composed of several Legionaries and a few tirailleurs.

As Bo-Ha is only about 7 miles from Nha-Nam, entailing a march of hardly two hours, and a journey in a native boat would be a new and desirable experience to me, I did not regret the delay this unexpected development was likely to create. I had not long to wait, however, for three days later our little fleet of twenty-five sampans, four of them occupied by the escort, glided away at three in the afternoon on its voyage up the river.

These sampans are about 20 feet long, and in form somewhat resemble a house-boat, though they are smaller and possess finer lines than the floating villas one meets with on the reaches of our English rivers during the summer months. The little house, or cabin, which is placed amidships in each of these boats, is usually about 6 feet by 5, and is so low that one can only sit or lie down inside it. Forward of this cabin is a deck from which two natives work the long sweeps of hardwood. These boatmen row in a standing position, with their faces towards the bow of the boat. Aft of the cabin is a strip of deck about 3 feet long, and from that the stern rises up in much the same way as one sees them pictured in the old prints of ships in the time of the Armada. Upon this deck stands another boatman, who handles a long oar which trails behind, and with this he both rows and steers. These boats draw very little water—2 feet at the utmost, and that only when they are fully laden.

The evening was a beautiful one, so that I made the most of the journey, and lay for several hours, my loaded rifle beside me, enjoying the varied spectacle which was quite new to me. In the boat, besides myself and the three boatmen, were three tirailleurs, but these gave me no trouble, for, having consumed a big saucepanful of rice, they fell asleep on the deck, the cabin being nearly filled with tin cases, each containing thirty kilos of flour. The sleepers lay close together to obtain more warmth, for the nights were chilly at this season.

The river at this part was from 80 to a 100 yards wide; its water was very clear, and ran over a sandy bottom, studded here and there with large rocks, and between steep banks, from 20 to 25 feet high.

Along either side ran groves of tall bamboos, which seemed to salute us with a graceful nod as we glided by. Sometimes there was a break, and an old pagoda, with a quaintly-curved roof of red-brown tiles, came into view. Now the river would run through a few miles of forest and jungle, offering no sign of occupation by man. Enormous trees rose superbly from the banks of the stream, and their massive branches extended for many feet over its waters, on which their foliage threw a pleasant and picturesque shadow. From these great limbs hung numerous flexible creepers, some of them starred with orchid-like blooms of white and yellow hue. Many of these streamers swayed gently to and fro before the light breeze, while others, having grown down into the glassy waters, were held still in their cool embrace.

Our journey between these walls of verdure, the forms and tints of which were ever changing, was one of the most delightful of experiences, the charm whereof is still fresh in my memory. When night came down and blotted out all colour and outline, I turned on to my back and watched the stars as they came out one by one. For an hour or so I lay open-eyed, yet dreaming, till the monotonous chant of our boatman, with its ever-recurring chorus of "Oh! Yah! Mōt-Haï-Ba!" finally lulled me into a profound slumber. Our convoy reached Bo-Ha in safety the following morning at nine.

This fort was constructed and garrisoned in 1889, at the request of a rich and influential native chief, lord of an important village, called Dao-Quan. This native was formerly a leader of a group of bandits, and, before the invasion of the country by the French, had ravaged the Yen-Thé and defied the mandarins in Bac-Ninh. After the capture of that citadel by the troops under General de Négrier, he was wise enough to throw in his lot with the invaders, and with his irregulars he fought side by side with his new allies against the old régime. In recognition of his services to the French cause, the Government confirmed his right to administer the district he had settled in, and made him a knight of the Legion of Honour. During the years that followed the occupation of the country by the French, he remained faithful to the cause he had adopted, and refused to have anything to do with the mandarins at the court at Hué, who were, in secret, partisans of the exiled Ham-Nghi, notwithstanding many overtures and rich promises made to him. During the operations in the Yen-Thé he rendered valuable service to the military authorities by supplying coolies to the different columns, and by making use of the armed irregulars, whom he maintained at his own expense, to guard the lines of communication. After the campaign was terminated he successfully negotiated the surrender of several influential minor chieftains, who, thanks to his efforts, came in and delivered up their arms.

We left Bo-Ha at two in the afternoon, our little troop consisting of a sergeant, three Legionaries, who were bound for Nha-Nam, with ten tirailleurs and a native corporal from the garrison we had left, the latter having been lent to strengthen our effective.

When we had marched for about half an hour and had crossed the Song-Soï, a little stream which runs into the Song-Thuong a few miles below Bo-Ha, we perceived, a hundred yards ahead of us, a small detachment, consisting of six tirailleurs, led by a European mounted on a native pony. I was one of the first to catch sight of them, for at the time I was in charge of the vanguard, which was composed of two natives. When we were close enough to get a good look at them, my surprise was great on recognising in the cavalier my friend Lipthay. When our mutual greetings and congratulations were over, he told me that he was out surveying the route with a view to determining the best positions for the poles of a telegraph line about to be established between Nha-Nam and the fort we had just left.

"I have done enough for to-day," said my chum, "and can easily finish the job in a couple of hours to-morrow morning. I will go and report to the sergeant, and come back to Nha-Nam with you."

A few minutes later he was riding beside me as I walked, and I was asking him many questions concerning all that had happened since I left, and as to when the operations were likely to begin; for now that he was on the District staff I knew he was likely to be well informed on these subjects.

"Well, things have been pretty lively during the last two months," he answered. "Captain Plessier has been keeping the company at Nha-Nam busy with reconnaissances and ambuscades, but there has been no serious engagement since the little affair at Long-Thuong, at which you were present. We made a grand coup at the beginning of last month, though, for we succeeded in finding a position rendering the enemy's big fort visible; a position on which it will not be difficult to place a battery of fieldguns, able to wish a better 'bonjour' to our rebel friends than those little toy pop-guns of the mountain artillery. What a pity old De-Nam is dead! He would have been so surprised when the first 90-millimètre shells came with a flop and a bang right into his secret lair; and from quite an unexpected quarter, too. Why——"

"Bon Dieu! mon ami," I interrupted, "have pity on me and go slow. Do you mean to say the old chief is dead?"

"Dead as Cæsar," answered my friend. "He was poisoned in October by some Chinese who came down from the north to sell arms and ammunition. They were his guests, and killed him because he won back all the money he had paid them at bacquang (a native game called fan-tan in Chinese). So the spies who came to Thaï-Nguyen told us. Dans tous les cas, he is dead, and was buried inside the big fort with great state; and De-Tam, his former lieutenant, is now commander-in-chief."

"But do you really mean to say that there is such a position as you have described?" I asked, for from my experience of the manner in which the rebels concealed their forts, such a thing seemed quite impossible.

"Most certainly," replied Lipthay. "I was on it, cher ami. But I had better tell you the tale from the beginning, for you matter-of-fact Englishmen are like St Thomas, and require palpable facts." He slipped his feet out of the stirrups, so that his long legs dangled comfortably, and, after shifting the carbine slung across his back into an easy position, began his tale.

"Towards the end of November, Linh-Nghi, the informer, was sent on to us at Thaï-Nguyen. You know the man, probably?" I nodded an affirmative, and he continued: "Et bien, Lieutenant Deleuze, chief of our Intelligence Department, used to pass hours at a time with him; took him to his house, and never lost sight of the fellow for a week. Deleuze speaks the vernacular like a native—pity there are so few like him—and the pair were soon like corps et chemise. I knew there was something brewing, and was not surprised when, on the 2nd December, orders were issued for a reconnaissance en force to proceed to Nha-Nam the following day. One company of the Legion and one of tirailleurs—a column 350 strong—and, of course, Deleuze and Linh-Nghi, were with them; so was I. Major Berard himself was in command. We slept a night at Nha-Nam, and went on to Bo-Ha the next day, after taking with us the mountain-gun from the former fort. At Bo-Ha we rested, and the following morning left by a path which runs to the north-west and passes through two ruined villages, Cho-Kai and Long-Ngo, which were burnt by Colonel Frey's column in January last."

"Why, you must have been due north of where the enemy's new positions are supposed to be!" I exclaimed.

"So you would think," said my friend; "but in reality we were due west. When we had got to a point about a kilomètre beyond where Cho-Kai used to be, the enemy's scouts, stationed on the hills to our left, signalled our advance by firing their rifles. Upon this the column left the path and made a general demonstration to the south-east. Our men got in touch with the enemy, and kept them occupied for a couple of hours by feinting an attack en règle. Lieutenant Deleuze and I took Linh-Nghi with us, and slipped quietly away to the west of the path. For an hour we scrambled along through the long grass, Nghi acting as guide. Then we went off to the north, walking all the time in the valleys, and keeping to the jungle so as to escape all chance of observation. At last we reached the foot of a hill somewhat taller than the surrounding ones—it was about 800 feet high—which had neither a bush nor a tree on its steep sides, but was covered all over with high, yellow grass. Nghi whispered that we must go cautiously to the top, so up we crawled on our hands and knees and lay flat on our stomachs when we reached the summit. Then we crept along until the opposite crest was gained. We had all brought big native hats with us, which we were careful to wear. When I looked down I was surprised to see that the path to Bo-Ha ran round the foot of this hill, and our column might have come here with ease, had it not been that this would have given the enemy some idea of what we were looking for. The view was a splendid one. First about 500 mètres of tall grass and jungle, then a kilomètre of forest which ran down to the Song-Soï, for we could catch here and there the gleam of its waters; beyond this a mass of hills thickly wooded, then more hills covered with grass, and beyond, bright green blotches of cultivated land.

"The weather was so clear that I caught sight of the flag at Nha-Nam, though it was quite 12 kilomètres away, and I pointed it out to Deleuze. Linh-Nghi stretched out his hand towards the forest, and, indicating a spot close to a bend in the little river, exclaimed excitedly: 'Look! look!' As I turned to him it seemed to me that his face was drawn and yellow, and his eyes were much brighter than usual. I could see nothing in the direction he pointed to but trees; but the lieutenant, after looking through his field-glasses for more than a minute, suddenly exclaimed: 'Sapristi! oui—I see roofs!' I turned to ask Nghi a question, but refrained from speaking, for he lay with his head on his arms, his face to the earth. He was sobbing like a child, and his heaving shoulders betokened the depth of his emotion."

"Poor devil!" I interrupted.

"Yes—poor devil," repeated Lipthay; then he continued: "Deleuze passed me his glasses, and after careful searching I caught glimpses of brown thatched roofs between the trees. These belonged to the houses within the big fortified village which has been in existence for three years at least. It is situated in the dense forest at a point where the Song-Soï forms a loop. So well is it concealed that had not Linh-Nghi been with us, I am convinced we should have failed to make it out. After a few minutes our native friend got the better of his emotion, and he started giving more explanations to the lieutenant concerning the position. While he was doing so I got out my peigne (a military surveying compass), sighted the flag at Nha-Nam, and got a bearing; then I obtained an angle on the Nuï-Dot—you know, the hill to the south-west of Nha-Nam, where they have fixed up a heliographic station. Time was getting on, and there was a danger of being sighted at any moment, so we crawled down the way we had come, hurried back to the column and reported. I fancy the Major was very glad to see us again, and I am sure he must have been pleased with the information Deleuze gave him.

"The troops were called in, and the column formed up on the path and marched back to Do-IIa. I don't think the enemy had an inkling of what we were after, and they were probably disappointed at not having succeeded in drawing our troops on into the forest, where they could have adopted their favourite tactics.

"Comments were rife among our men, for they had counted on an engagement, and, as they expressed it: 'On a arrêté la danse au moment où les violons étaient accordés.' As we were marching away I heard one fellow say: 'Bon Dieu! bon Dieu! I don't believe the old fossil knows himself what we did go out for. They might just as well have sent a few recruits from the biff (the line regiments). Why, for three long hours we did nothing but waste our ammunition on half a dozen skinny natives who were dodging about among the trees.' Quel malheur! If they had known the result obtained, they would have sung another song; but it must be kept secret, of course, until the campaign is opened, and that will not be before the beginning of March."

"Rather late, isn't it?" I asked.

"Well, you see, it will be fine and cold then," answered my friend; "and with the information we now possess I don't think the expedition ought to last more than a fortnight." He now gave me more details concerning the defensive organisation of the rebels.

Besides the big fortified village already mentioned, about 4 miles to the north of Hou-Thué (demolished by Colonel Frey's column a year before), there were numerous positions, forts and entrenchments built to defend the paths leading to it. All these obstacles were accumulated to the south and east of the main position, from which it was evident that the rebels were confident that all future attacks would come from the same direction as the preceding ones.

De-Tam possessed a force of about two thousand men, twelve hundred of whom were armed with breech loading rifles of various patterns.

It was also probable that this chief was aware that the French would commence operations against him, as soon as the weather was cool enough to allow of large bodies of European troops being moved about the country, and that in consequence he had come to some understanding with the powerful leaders of the Chinese bands in North and West Tonquin, so as to secure their assistance in case of need. Of these, the two most important were Ba-Ky and Luong-Tam-Ky, who occupied vast tracts of mountainous country to the north of the Yen-Thé, into which the French had, as yet, made no serious effort to penetrate. Both of these brigand chieftains had established their domination in these districts some time before the arrival of the Western foreigners in Tonquin.

Colonel—now General—Frey in his admirable work on the subject, compares them to the feudal lords of the Middle Ages, since they administered the territory occupied as a fief, all the inhabitants being subjected to regular taxation, wisely calculated so as not to excite discontent, and their authority was undisputed. These two leaders could dispose of from two to three thousand Chinese, armed with rifles, part of which force they would certainly be willing to place at the service of De-Tam on the payment of a stipulated sum of money. In fact, this is what actually did happen. Ba-Ky and Luong-Tam-Ky submitted to French rule in 1895, but their territory has not been occupied by the troops, for two very good reasons: first, because the district is so poor that the expense entailed would hardly be justifiable, and also owing to the fact that the region is so unhealthy that Europeans cannot remain there any length of time without falling victims to fever and dysentery.

When we reached Nha-Nam, I received a hearty greeting from my comrades, some of whom, owing to my prolonged absence, were under the impression that I had also fallen a victim to the Cho-Trang fever, as they called it. It was comforting to find myself back in my former quarters, to fall once more into the jargon of the corps and take part in the daily routine of the garrison.

Two days later Lipthay left for Thaï-Nguyen with Lieutenant Deleuze. I saw this smart intelligence officer. He was a small, brown-faced, wiry man, whose most remarkable trait was the quiet, low toned voice in which he spoke to those under him. The men told wild tales concerning his wonderful knowledge of the language and customs of the natives, whereby, it was said, he had on several occasions been able to adopt a disguise, and accompany some of the native spies on their expeditions. Whether this was exact or not I should not like to declare, but it is certain that this officer possessed a wonderful knowledge of the vernacular, and was a topographical expert of no small merit.

I had hardly time to settle down in my old quarters again, for a week after my arrival my section was sent off to Bo-Ha to strengthen the garrison in that part, which at the time consisted of a company of native troops under the orders of Captain Perrin.

One night, shortly after our arrival there—it was the 16th January, 1892—the section was suddenly called out, orders being given for each man to take with him a flannel suit, rolled up in his waterproof blanket—which was slung across the chest—and provisions for two days. We soon learned that a long night's march lay before us; for a wire had been received from the Brigade, to the effect that a portion of Ba-Ky's band was marching on Cho-Trang with the intention of rushing that outpost, and our orders were to get there as soon as possible by the nearest way. A guide was supplied by the headman of Dao-Quan, who led us away by a track slanting off to the north east of Bo-Ha, across a wild, uncultivated region, hitherto little explored, and generally considered impracticable.

We started off at eleven, and it was easy walking for the first mile or so, but once we had left behind us the cultivated district surrounding our fort, the path went from bad to worse. We passed for several miles over a plain covered with jungle, after which the track went into the hills, and, though we kept up the pace, it was terrible work as we went now up, now down, then splashing through the icy cold water of the little streams coursing down each valley. Though the night was fairly clear it was dark, and difficult to see ahead in the gullies and dips, and we had to trust to luck sometimes when putting our foot forward.

We reached Cho-Phang, a Muong village, at a quarter past three in the morning, and a pedometer which I carried registered 18½ miles. We had now gained the rocky chain of the Nui-Dong-Nai, and thence the path ran along at the foot of these heights. We rested a quarter of an hour, and then continued our hurried tramp till we reached the Deo-Mou-Phieu pass, concerning which I have already written when describing my first journey to Cho-Trang. We passed through the cleft, going due north, and reached our destination at a few minutes past seven.

This was the hardest march it has ever been my lot to undertake, and, as already stated, we covered close upon 32 miles in about eight hours. The garrison—they were tirailleurs, for the detachment of the Legion had left more than a month before—was on the alert when we arrived, but had seen no sign of brigands. We were all glad to get inside the fort and take a few hours' rest. During the morning a telegram was received, stating that the band had taken another direction, and that all danger was passed. Desiring, no doubt, that we should not pass the night in so unhealthy a region, Captain Perrin, who had come with us, started us on our way back at two in the afternoon. We went at a moderate speed, passing the night at Cho-Thuong, where there are some wonderful caves, the entrance to which is some 60 feet from the ground. In these some of us tried to sleep, but were driven away by a host of parasites. Access was gained to these caverns by means of long bamboo ladders. When their village, which is situated at the base of the rock, is attacked by bandits, the Muongs take refuge with their women and children in these caves, where, after hoisting up the ladders, they are absolutely secure from attack. Strange to say, they succeed in getting their cattle into these shelters in time of danger, but whether they do so by the aid of ropes, or through some lower entrance known only to themselves, I was unable to ascertain.

We reached Bo-Ha at three in the afternoon on the following day.

During the next few weeks our detachment was kept very busy preparing things for the troops, which were soon to be concentrated at this point; and we spent a considerable part of our time working at the road from the landing-stage on the Song-Thuong up to the fort. This had to be widened and levelled so as to allow of the passage of field artillery.

It was very evident that the rebels were alive to the fact that operations against them were intended, for their vedettes were continually in evidence round Bo-Ha and Nha-Nam, and along the road between these forts. No movement could be made by the troops of these two garrisons without it being at once signalled by the enemy's scouts. Their methods for communicating information at a distance were really ingenious. By day they made use of a code of smoke signals, to obtain which torches composed of chopped straw, resin and gunpowder were used; at night oil lanterns with a sliding shutter attachment, or paper balloons carrying a burning rag soaked in petroleum, served the same purpose.

Stores and ammunition continued to arrive, so that temporary sheds had to be erected outside the fort, for the go-downs inside were filled to overflowing.

On the 5th and 6th March a company of the Legion from Lang-son, a battalion of Infanterie de Marine, one of Tirailleurs Tonkinois, a company of engineers, a battery of field artillery, one of mountain-guns (in all, two thousand five hundred men and twelve guns), and two thousand coolies arrived at Bo-Ha. These men, who were lodged in huts constructed of bamboo and macaw-palm, composed the first column, destined to march to the north-east and seize the hill, which had been the subject of Lipthay's discourse to me on my return from Quang-Yen, whence they would be able to attack the enemy from quite an unexpected quarter. At Nha-Nam a second column, composed of five companies of the Legion, a battalion of Infanterie de Marine, three companies of native troops, a battery of mountain guns and two mortars (two thousand eight hundred men and eight guns), was concentrated, preparatory to advancing in two groups, from the south-west, along the paths already thoroughly explored by the troops operating against Hou-Thué in the preceding year.

From Thaï-Nguyen a third force, consisting of two companies of the Legion, three of tirailleurs (one thousand and fifty men), and two mountain-guns, was to march from the west, thus striking the rebels' right flank, and joining hands with the column from Bo-Ha.

The loyal Delta provinces supplied about one thousand irregulars armed with rifles, and these, officered by their local military mandarins, had orders to cover the flanks of the different columns, and, whenever possible, maintain communication between them. A French officer was detached to control their movements.

On the 8th March General Voyron arrived at Bo-Ha with his staff, and a council-of-war was held at which all the commanders of columns and groups were present. When the General had exposed his plan of campaign, each of the officers present was provided with printed instructions concerning the tactics to be adopted, particular stress being laid on the recommendation to abstain from delivering attacks on fortified positions, unless a careful preparation for the assault had been made by artillery fire. Great enthusiasm prevailed among the soldiers of the Legion, and all were burning with a desire to be in at the finish, the men of my company being particularly keen, which is easily comprehensible, since for more than a year this unit had been continually aux prises with the enemy, and there were comrades to avenge, and sleepless nights and long marches to make good. The old soldiers were impressed by the elaborate preparations that had been made and the strength of the force employed, and they were unanimous in the opinion that this time the "Valorous and Invincible Battalions," as De-Tam pompously styled his troops, would be scattered to the four corners of Tonquin, and their lairs would become the haunt of the tiger, the panther and the bear. It is also probable that a good many of the Legionaries secretly cherished the hope of doing a little looting "on their own," for wild tales had been circulated concerning vast treasures secreted somewhere within the precincts of De-Nam's house, now occupied by his successor.

Next day two battalions of infantry and the battery of mountain-guns left Bo-Ha, and, after a forced march, occupied the hill already mentioned, which to facilitate orders was designated as Point A. As soon as this position was securely held the engineers got to work, prepared the track leading to it and cut a zigzag road up the flank of the hill to its summit, so as to permit of the heavier artillery being brought up. A thousand coolies worked with the sappers, and the task of preparing about 6 miles of road and cutting a path up the sugar-loafed hill was completed in a little over forty-eight hours; so that on the evening of the 13th a battery of six guns was established on the top of Point A, and the whole of the column, with its reserve of stores and ammunition, was entrenched at its base. The light field fortifications necessary to shelter this force were made by the infantry with the aid of the entrenching tools each soldier carried.

During these four days the enemy had not been idle, for their skirmishers maintained a constant fire on the column, the workers on the road and the passing convoys, and we suffered some casualties in consequence. At night their snipers claimed a few victims, but up to this phase of the operations the losses on our side were few.

At this time my section was chiefly employed in escorting the convoys from Bo-Ha to Point A, or in covering the working parties on the road. We sometimes slept in the fort, and sometimes in the camp with the column: this depending on which of these two places was nearest to us at the end of the day. We had several slight brushes with the enemy's scouts, none of which, however, were of any importance.

In the camp, when not on duty, I was glad to wander around from one bivouac to another. In the French infantry lines things were generally quiet, and these young soldiers, who had passed most of their time in the colony, in the garrison towns, were evidently out of their element. Most of them, when questioned on the subject, openly expressed their desire that the operations might be of very short duration, though these troops were undoubtedly as brave as their ancestors who fought at Fontenoy, Jemappes or Jena, and had the call on their patriotism been made for a supreme effort in Europe, they would have hailed the chance with enthusiasm. As it was, the prospect was one of a violent end, by the hand of an unseen foe, in some dark corner of the tropical jungle, and this to further a colonial policy in which few of them felt either interest or confidence. The ever-existing danger from the deadly malaria, the distance separating them from their patrie and their homes, and the thought that their presence was due to the brutal hazard and ill-luck attached to conscription: these were reasons hardly conducive to a liking for the hardships and risks of the campaign. Not that the morale or courage of these troops was in the least affected by this state of things, but their dislike for the expedition was evident and outspoken.

With the Legionaries it was different, and their bivouac echoed with the rollicking choruses sung by the men as they sat around the fires. Between songs they would crack jokes at each other's expense, and enter into friendly discussions as to who would be the next to "eat bananas by the roots," which was their playful way of suggesting a hurried burial in soft soil. These were grown men, vigorous and hardened, and therefore better able to resist fever, fatigue and privation than the youthful conscripts, their neighbours, who sat by the blaze and talked in subdued tones of "la chaumière et les vieux" in sunny France. The Legionary possesses a rude but kindly nature, and, like the soldier of fortune that he is, he revels in the adventurous existence he has adopted, the hazards and dangers of it being the wine of life to him. Without desire for honour or reward, without even the wish that their deeds should receive public attention, these condotieri of to-day perform incredible feats of daring and devotion. Professional soldiers they are, and they will remain unmoved by brilliant discourses concerning the glory and honour of war, except that they will express their contempt for such speeches by an occasional wink and a smile at their neighbour in the ranks. For they love deeds, not words, and, when led by an officer who possesses their confidence and whose courage is undisputed, they will be generously, almost foolishly, heroic, going to meet death with light-hearted gaiety, laying down their lives for him without a murmur.

The native troops were not unworthy of interest. Squatting round their fires on various pieces of matting they had procured from no one knew where, their turbans removed and their long hair falling almost to their waists, they agitated the paper fans, which each of them usually carried thrust in his belt, thus driving away the mosquitoes swarming around. Their small hands, beardless faces, and rolling walk as they moved about, and the quiet, singing drawl in which they spoke, left on the observer an impression that they were effeminate. It was hard to realise that under this gentle exterior these natives possessed a talent for cruelty and cunning to a degree attained by few other races. The causes and probable results of the campaign were of small importance to them, if one could judge by the mask of Oriental indifference they wore, though it was hard indeed to learn their real sentiments on any subject, for it was rarely that they betrayed their inner thoughts to a European, even though he knew their language and could converse with them. The value of these troops as a military unit is a question that has been treated in a preceding chapter.

At 6 a.m. on the 14th the battery on the hill opened a hot fire with a salvo of shrapnel aimed at what was supposed to be the centre of the fortified village; the distance given by the range-finders being 2800 mètres. The bombardment was kept up, the guns being trained at various distances so as to sweep the position and its surroundings, till nine that morning, when a dense mist rose from the intervening forest and obscured the target.

Clouds of damp vapour hung about the trees during the remainder of the day, so that all action of the guns was out of the question.

Profiting by the cover offered by the fog, the Commander-in-Chief sent out several companies of infantry towards the enemy's position, in the hope of ascertaining whether the artillery had succeeded in damaging the fortifications. The passage of these troops through the forest was opposed by the rebel skirmishers, who, however, retired into the fort when the attack was pressed home. The columns pushed forward towards the enemy's defences, the men being instructed to go slowly and take all the cover available, and it was discovered that from this side glimpses of the ramparts could be obtained at a distance of a little under 100 mètres, which was considerably more advantageous to the attacking force than had been the case at Hou-Thué, where all forward movements were executed in the dark, since the position was not visible until the assaulting troops were right upon it. This important information obtained, the reconnaissance retired, without, however, having been able to determine to what extent the fire of the guns had been effective. That same morning the second column left Nha-Nam in two groups, and, driving the enemy before them, proceeded slowly and cleared the country up to Long-Thuong and Dinh-Tep, where they halted for the night.

The force from Thaï-Nguyen also started on its way, to find itself opposed, after a march of 18 miles, by Ba-Ky's Chinese, who were entrenched in considerable force close to Mona-Luong. The first position on the road was assaulted and captured by the Legion, which suffered several losses, but inflicted severe punishment on the enemy. This column camped on the site of its success, and passed the night there. Thus the first day of active operations had been a successful one, and the advance had been general along the line of attack.

On the 15th March, the weather being fine and clear, it was found possible to renew the bombardment, and a slow, searching fire was kept up all day. In all about two thousand shells were thrown into the enemy's position.

The troops skirmished towards the fortifications, and, behind them, the engineers and coolies, with the aid of axe and saw, cleared a broad track through the forest. Dynamite was used to level the big trees, giants of the jungle, in dealing with which ordinary methods would have been too long and laborious. Towards evening a position was reached, about 200 yards from the ramparts, whence a good view of the defences could be obtained, and offering to a mountain battery a fair chance of effecting a breach. The column from Nha-Nam made slow but steady progress during the day, and succeeded in driving the enemy from several forts and entrenchments.

The force from Thaï Nguyen also effected a cautious and successful advance, shelling and capturing trench after trench. Just before sunset we could hear their little mountain-guns hammering away at the retreating army. Before night fell a message was flashed from this column stating that it had reached a point on the road leading to our position, about 8 miles distant.

During the day the losses on our side had been small compared with the progress made; and since the commencement of the operations the total casualties of the expedition amounted to ten killed and thirty-two wounded. It was certain that the enemy had suffered severely, for more than forty of their dead had been found in and around the different positions captured.

My section had been on camp-guard duty all day, much to the disgust of all of us, and, to pass away the time when not on sentry-go, I climbed up the hill and watched events. From this position the sight was a grand one, for, as I have said, a panorama of the whole region could be obtained.

Crossing the brush-covered plain, going to and fro between the forest—that hid the enemy and our attacking force—and our camp situated at the base of the hill on which I stood, was a constant stream of humanity. Now it was a gang of coolies, under charge of a sapper, going to relieve some of their comrades who were clearing a way for the guns: then a string of more of these useful but ragged and dirty auxiliaries, trotting along in couples with a long bamboo between them, on which were suspended boxes of rifle ammunition. From the forest came a little convoy of wounded, or dead—who could tell from here? For the naked eye could just distinguish three crumpled, reclining figures, each covered with a brown army blanket, lying on the stretchers which the ambulance men carried carefully over the obstacles in their path. One of the three groups formed by the stretchers and their bearers suddenly stopped, and the burden was gently lowered to the ground. I saw a man run off to the right, something at the end of a strap swinging from his right hand, and suddenly I realised that this balancing object was a water-bottle. A kindly artillery sergeant, whose gun, close to where I had been standing, had just vomited a shell, handed me his field-glasses with a smile, and with a salute I thanked him for having guessed my eager desire. When I had adjusted the glasses, the soldier was back by the stretcher, and kneeling beside it was supporting his wounded friend's head with one hand, while with the other he held to the poor fellow's lips the flask containing the precious liquid he had been craving for. Only those who have been wounded can form a true idea of the terrible thirst that seizes hold of a man who has been stricken down; water is like new life to him, for all his anatomy seems parched up, burning, and the friend who can procure it is an angel of mercy indeed. I recognised in the wounded man and his chum two privates from the 3rd Company of the Legion, despatched from Lang-son to assist in the operations. The "parrakeet brigade" we laughingly styled them, because their brave but somewhat eccentric captain had seen fit to dress them in green drill, which he declared made his men less visible at a distance than the conventional khaki. One of the men, the stricken one, was a Prussian; his comrade an Alsatian: hereditary enemies, if some political historians are to be believed, but here there was no room for race-hatred. There was no thought of it in the Legion, and surely no better demonstration could be given of the fact than the little incident I have described. Now the belated stretcher was moving on towards a big tent situated in a corner of the camp, from the top of which floated a red-cross flag. This was the field hospital, in which the head surgeon, M. de Camprieu, and his staff of doctors and orderlies were very busy; for besides the wounded there were numerous cases of fever and dysentery to be attended to.

With the glasses I tried to pierce the shadows of the forest, but the foliage was too thick, and the only indications of the struggle that was going on there under its vast roof of leaves, and between its serried tree-trunks, were the occasional puffs of smoke filtering through the verdure, the distant rat! tat! tat! of the rifles, punctuated now and again by a sharp crack of an exploding dynamite cartridge as it splintered the massive bole of a banyan or teak.

I handed back the glasses to the kindly "non-com," and watched the artillerymen working the guns. They were firing slowly now, one a minute. A captain, standing behind the centre of the line of long-necked, vicious-looking field-pieces, gave the command: "Première pièce ... feu!" "Bang!" howled the ugly war-dog as it skidded back a yard on its locked wheels, and from the distant forest came back the sharp crack of the bursting shell, easily distinguished from the other reports arising from the wood.

The rebels were not the only sufferers from the guns, for the continued detonations had driven from their usual haunts the herds of deer which frequented the region, and in consequence the tigers, missing their prey, were prowling about empty and enraged. At night their weird "cop! cop! cop!" occasional snarl, or gruesome roar would waken the stillness of the jungle, as they roamed around our camp; and on several occasions I experienced an uncomfortable icy feeling from the back of the neck downwards when these sounds approached me during my two hours of sentry-go in the dark. Our column lost two coolies and three commissariat bullocks, both men and cattle being carried away by these "striped devils," as the natives called them. A tirailleur sentry belonging to the Thaï-Nguyen force also fell a victim to their hunger.

On the 16th a general attack was made by all our columns, and though the results of the day's work were favourable—for we had succeeded in establishing a mountain battery in a sheltered position within a short distance of the rebel ramparts, and the force from Thai-Nguyen, after brushing aside all resistance and capturing a big fort at Mo-Trang, the existence of which was previously unknown, had joined hands with us—yet this success was marred, early in the day, by a costly disaster, overtaking one of the groups composing the southeastern column. This unit, which was commanded by a major, only escaped complete destruction and the loss of its artillery by little short of a miracle. The two guns attached to the group got stuck in a swampy rice field when coming to the assistance of the infantry, who had walked into the close and unexpected fire of an enemy strongly entrenched on a steep hill covered with dense vegetation. For some unknown reason the commander ordered the surprised and somewhat disorganised troops to assault the position. An attempt was made to execute this order, but it was unsuccessful, and the column suffered severe loss, two officers and twenty-six men being killed, and one officer and thirty-two men wounded. A company of Legionaries who were scouting in the neighbourhood fortunately created a diversion by attacking the rear of the enemy's position, and this allowed what remained of the little column, principally composed of French infantry and tirailleurs, to retire in comparative safety with their guns. Unfortunately, a certain number of the slain were left behind among the trees on the side of the hill, and these, with their rifles and ammunition, fell into the hands of the enemy. The officer responsible for this gross blunder was sent back to Hanoï, pending an enquiry, and the incident cast a passing gloom over the operations.

Though this partial success somewhat revived the already ebbing courage of De-Tam's tried and devoted veterans, large numbers of his less enthusiastic supporters were continually breaking away from his little army, and gliding between our outposts, for it was impossible to establish with the troops at the disposal of our leader a complete cordon in a district so vast and offering such good cover. Some of these small bands made their way to the south, and found refuge in the friendly villages of the lower Yen-Thé; others went north, and obtained security in the territories occupied by the Chinese chief.

The following day saw the downfall of the enemy's central position, for, after a bombardment of three hours by the guns on Point A and by the mountain batteries of the different columns, which were now on three sides of it, the defences were rushed at two points, at three in the afternoon. Though I took part in this final assault, it is hardly necessary to describe in detail the fighting. Suffice it that the rout of De-Tam's force was complete.

Once inside the fortifications one and all were struck by the immense amount of labour and skill that had been expended on their construction. The colonel in command of the artillery during the operations stated in his report that it might be roughly estimated that at least fifteen hundred coolies, working continually during nine months, must have been employed to complete these defences. The superficial area of the interior of the position was about one square mile, and upon it more than a hundred constructions had been erected, consisting of lodgings for the chiefs, barracks for the men, huts for the women and children, two fine pagodas and a big grain-store, raised from the ground on stone pillars, and containing more than 500 tons of rice when the position fell into our hands. The ramparts were splendidly constructed, and in some places three lines of marksmen, placed one above the other, could find protection behind them, being sheltered from the artillery fire by casemates. On three sides the Song-Soï served as a moat to the fort, while on the fourth a canal had been cut for the same purpose.

The enemy suffered great loss during the final development of the attack, and numerous were the bodies strewn all over their position, or hurriedly buried in the banana and areca-palm plantations surrounding some of their houses.

As an example to all insurgents, and also to put a stop to the dangerous and superstitious legends in circulation concerning the supernatural powers of De-Nam, the body of this chief was disinterred, and his remains scattered to the four winds. The skull of the famous rebel is now in the possession of a military doctor of high rank.

Unfortunately De-Tam, together with a few of his most faithful supporters, succeeded in making good his escape from the fort shortly before the troops entered. Though this chief was never again able to organise rebellion on such an elaborate scale, he nevertheless gave great trouble to the French authorities, and inflicted severe losses on the troops sent against him during the next five years.

The most important part of the operations against the Yen-Thé rebels was now terminated. During the following week the columns, split up into groups, made regular battues through the forests and jungle of the region, and many more of the rebels were captured or slain. There can be no doubt that the success of the expedition, the rapid downfall of the numerous strong positions, and the penetration by the French troops into that mysterious region—the soil of which, the natives had been led to believe, would never be violated by the foot of the Western foreigner—produced a lasting and beneficial effect on the minds of the whole of the population of Tonquin, and did more to impress on them the fact that the domination of the country by the French was irrevocable and definite, than thousands of printed manifestoes bearing the name of a President, or a Governor-General whose importance was small in the eyes of the Annamese when compared with the lustre attached to their exiled monarch.

Several of the minor chiefs, recognising the futility of further resistance, came in with their men and surrendered to the authorities in Nha-Nam and Bo-Ha; in this way, during the fortnight that followed the capture of their positions, the rebels brought in nearly two hundred rifles.

About five hundred of the enemy, who had succeeded in getting away to the south, established themselves in several villages near Dap-Cau, and pillaged the surrounding country. Their success was short-lived, however, for, though the majority of the troops were now being sent back to their respective garrisons, two thousand men and two guns were sent against them under the orders of Lieutenant-Colonel Geil, and a fortnight later, owing to the skilful tactics of this officer, the flickering embers of revolt in the lower Yen-Thé were stamped out, and the supporters of the movement scattered or slain.

CHAPTER VII

The remnants of the rebel forces, which had been smashed and dispersed by Colonel Geil's column in the lower Yen-Thé, fled north and rallied round their chief, De-Tam, who was hiding, together with a small number of his most trusted retainers, in one of the wildest spots in the dense forest region of the north-west of Nha-Nam, and about 10 miles from that fort. This district is known to the natives by the name of Quinh-Low.

At this time, owing to the large number of rebels we had slain or captured, or who had surrendered during the past two months, the total number of insurgents with De-Tam did not exceed two hundred. Efforts had been made by the provincial mandarins to secure the chieftain's submission. The French Government, preferring, if possible, to adopt a policy of conciliation, rather than run the risks and be burdened with the heavy expense resulting from a protracted struggle with such a brave, resourceful and mobile foe, authorised the native functionaries to offer the leader of the insurrection not only his life and liberty, but also a remunerative post in the local administration, on the condition that he would come in with his men and deliver up his arms and ammunition.

These negotiations fell through, however, for De-Tam refused all offers made to him, and wrote several letters to the French authorities in which he informed them, in his usual high-flown, bombastic style, that he would never surrender, and that he still possessed the utmost confidence in the ultimate success of the cause he represented. Notwithstanding these assertions, it is very probable that he would gladly have accepted the terms offered had he been certain of enjoying a quiet and comfortable life after his capitulation; but he was too well versed in the natural cunning of his race not to know full well that, in the event of his surrender, his very existence would be a cause of constant dread to his former associates, the mandarins of the Court of Hué, and they would most certainly find a way of ensuring his silence, by means both wily and rapid, in the use of which Orientals are experts.

From papers captured by the French troops, when they surprised the encampment at Quinh-Low a few weeks later, it was learnt that the chief had decided on the construction of a new series of defensive positions in this region, with the intention of carrying on the rebellion with something like its former success. His desires in this respect were, however, doomed to disappointment, for such was the constant activity of the troops occupying the different parts in the upper Yen-Thé that no rest or respite were allowed him or his men. When the main expedition had been broken up at the end of March, General Voyron had given orders for the permanent occupation of the fortified positions at Mo-Trang and Mona-Luong. These two forts, which had both been captured from the enemy by the Thaï-Nguyen column, were well constructed, and they required but little labour, mainly in the direction of felling the trees that were too close up to the ramparts, to make them almost impregnable when properly garrisoned. For several months after the conclusion of the principal operations, the troops from these two forts, together with the men from Nha-Nam and Bo-Ha, chased De-Tam from one hiding-place to another; and, in consequence, he was never able to establish any permanent centre of resistance.

Early in May my section was relieved by a similar detachment of the Legion from Thaï-Nguyen, and we left Bo-Ha—for good this time—and returned to our company at Nha-Nam.

On the 10th of the same month we were assembled under arms to witness the departure of Captain Plessier, who was leaving for Haïphong, whence he sailed for France a few days later. Our new commander, Captain Watrin, took over the company and escorted his predecessor as far as Cao-Thuong. Though the officer who was leaving us had always been a severe disciplinarian, unsparing in regard to the work he had required of us, yet his departure was a cause of chagrin to his Legionaries; and their rough, though heartfelt expressions of regret were numerous and outspoken. None of the officers are allowed to remain more than three consecutive years in Tonquin, though they can return there after a sojourn with their regiment in Algeria. Our Captain had completed his period of colonial service, so that he could not have remained longer with us even had he desired so to do. Officers of his stamp, that is, men whose bravery is undisputed, who are severe but also anxious for the welfare of the troops under their orders, will always be popular with the Legionaries. His successor eventually became an even greater favourite with the company, for, besides the qualities mentioned already, he had a real affection for his men, though, when the occasion required it, he tempered this sentiment with necessary sternness. He regarded his command as a family, of which he was proud to be the head, and made no show of the taciturn aloofness which had characterised his predecessor. Captain Watrin, who was about thirty-eight years of age, was a splendid specimen of humanity, for he was tall, broad-shouldered, and extremely powerful. Fair, with blue eyes and a ruddy complexion, he was a typical son of the "Lost Provinces"; and the fact of his being a native of a village near Strassburg added not a little to his popularity with the numerous Alsatians in the company. He seemed to take a real pleasure in making himself acquainted with the individual joys and sorrows of his men. Whenever the chance offered itself, he would question us discreetly concerning our private hopes and ambitions, and do his best to prove to his subordinates that he was to them not only a chief, inflexible as far as questions of discipline were concerned, but also a friend to whom they could confide their troubles, ever ready with a word of consolation or advice, and all the aid it lay in his power to render. His enquiries were probably distasteful to such of the men as possessed a past they did not care to recall; but when he perceived that a private was reluctant to confide in him, he was too tactful to insist on the subject, and would smooth matters over by a cheerful, "Et bien, mon brave. When you want a confessor, come to me. I may perhaps be able to help you."

A few weeks after his arrival he was able to address every private in his company by name, a trait which is exceedingly rare with the officers in the French army. There is no doubt that the men were very grateful to him for this detail, which certainly proved that their chief was aware the Legionary was not merely an enfant perdu, to be known only by the number stamped on each article of his kit, but that he recognised that his men, like the rest of mankind, possessed their just share of pride and passion, vice and virtue.

He very soon showed us that his military talents were of sterling quality, for in his first engagements with the enemy it was at once evident that his dispositions for the attack were taken with great coolness and forethought, and with the careful intention of avoiding all wanton loss of life. During the final rush and scrimmage he was ever to the fore, and would not be denied the place of honour at the head of the assault, which he led with no other weapon than a thick stick.

Our company was kept continually on the move during the months of May and June, reconnaissances and ambuscades being of daily occurrence. Often we would make a night march, and, operating in conjunction with parties sent out from the other forts, rush at dawn a village in which several of the rebels had passed the night, or capture an encampment situated in some out-of-the-way corner of the forest, or hidden in a narrow jungle-covered defile between tall, steep hills.

Our ambuscades were generally placed on the paths leading to the south by which supplies, coming from the few isolated villages still friendly to the rebel cause, reached the enemy. These expeditions always took place at night, for our foes no longer possessed the strength and confidence which had allowed them to move about the country by day, as they had been in the habit of doing before the downfall of their citadels. To the majority of us the excitement of these little expeditions was a source of real joy, notwithstanding the dose of fever or twinge of rheumatism that sometimes resulted. We enjoyed the silent, stealthy march through the dark, the long wait, hidden in rank jungle, with anxious eyes peering through the gloom, our fingers on the trigger, all listening intently to the thousand soft noises of the night. Every nerve would be strained to its utmost tension, every faculty keenly on the alert. The rustle of the long grass as a deer or wild hog moved cautiously through it, the breaking of a twig, the hoot of an owl, or even the sudden shrill chirp of the cicala would make the heart leap with expectation, so that its hurried throb sent the blood coursing through the arteries, and the system would tingle again under a wave of suppressed excitement. More often than not our expectation would be disappointed, for the enemy failed to put in an appearance, though now and again our patience would be rewarded by a scrimmage, and a convoy would be captured and several rebels slain or taken. Once our ambuscade was surrounded and suddenly rushed by a strong band of most determined Chinese banditti, of whose presence in the region we were unaware. It is probable that they were going south with a convoy of contraband opium. A desperate hand-to-hand struggle took place in the dark. One of our men was killed in the first charge, and several were wounded. One of the latter, a bugler, died of his injuries a few days later. It is difficult to surmise what would have been the result of the combat had not another detachment of our men, which had been posted at a small ford about half a mile away, come to our assistance, for we were completely surrounded, and owing to the blackness of the night we could hardly distinguish our foes, who were cunning enough not to make use of their rifles, attacking us instead at close quarters with their heavy swords. On finding themselves charged in the rear the Celestials withdrew, and at daybreak we found six of their dead on or near the position. All these had been slain by the bayonet, for there had been but little firing on our side since, owing to the danger of shooting our friends, it had been found necessary to keep to steel. Though our adventure lasted only a few minutes, I think those of us who escaped unhurt from the mêlée were passing thankful when it was over; for never was it better proved that if in warfare an ambuscade can cause great hurt to an enemy who comes upon it unawares, that same ambuscade is in danger of total destruction should the enemy be forewarned of its presence.

At this time, thanks to the experience they had acquired during the past year and a half, and also to their having been employed during the last three months in continually chasing the enemy from place to place, through the wildest country it is possible to imagine, the men of my company had become splendid jungle fighters. Each of them was now not only a hardened, almost fever-proof soldier, but also a good shot and an efficient scout, ever on the alert to notice each sign by the way, to catch each sound in the air, and understand their meaning. A footprint, a broken twig, a tiny streak of smoke creeping up from between the trees to the sky, the dull thud of the distant axe as it hit the wood, and the hundred and one other trifling indications of the passage of man in the tangle of forest-covered hills were at once seized upon and put to profit.

Conversant with the enemy's methods of fighting in the dark glades and sombre thickets of his favourite haunts, the Legionaries and their officers had learnt to trust no longer to the paths, but to advance silently yet swiftly through the undergrowth, taking advantage of every bit of cover, and making of each tree in the wood, each rise in the ground, a temporary rampart. Encouraged by their officers, the men took great delight in this new sport, which seemed more like a hunt, in which the quarry was man, than regular warfare. The fact of their not being continually in touch with their officers and "non-coms," and having consequently to depend sometimes on their own resources, developed their individual initiative and self-reliance; whilst the novelty of the situation gave full scope to their courage and love of adventure. Perhaps with troops possessing less stamina and morale, even these short periods of independent action would have been dangerous, but with these well-disciplined and seasoned soldiers of the Legion this new method of attack seemed rather to increase the zeal and self-confidence of the men.

The following statement, drawn up by a rebel deserter, the written translation of which still exists, most probably, in the records at the headquarters of the 2nd Brigade, will give some idea of how hard pressed were De-Tam and his faithful few by our troops at this period.

"The favourite wife of our old chief De-Nam was heavy with child when the fire from the big guns and the approach of your infantry in such great numbers obliged us to evacuate our positions. Notwithstanding her condition she accompanied De-Tam and his lieutenants De-Truat and De-Hué into the great forest at Quinh-Low. Here she gave birth to a male child, posthumous son of our former leader; this was on the second day of the fifth month" (May 26th). "At this time there were but few men with De-Tam, for the majority of our troops had been scattered all over the country, and many had gone south to their villages; thus we were but sixty men armed with rifles, and with us were seven women and two little ones. We had plenty to eat, for we drew rice from the secret hiding-places in the forest, where great store of this food had been placed many months before, by the wise orders of our Ong (Lord), who was dead. But the white soldiers left us no peace, and each day they pressed us so hard that we dared not sleep two nights in the same place. At last we found a cave, to reach which we had to descend a passage leading straight down into the earth." (In this district are to be found numerous workings of former iron mines which were abandoned several centuries ago, and are now overgrown with jungle. It is probably to one of these that the deserter made allusion.) "We had been in hiding in this place for several days when a party of soldiers, who had followed the tracks of one of our men who had been sent out to fetch water, nearly discovered our retreat. These soldiers hunted for us until sundown and remained all the night in the forest, so that, knowing this and fearing lest the cries of the young child should betray us, De-Tam ordered us to dig a hole, and in it De-Nam's son was buried alive.

"When the mother was told of what had befallen her babe—for it had been taken from her whilst she was sleeping, and she knew not where it had gone—she was stricken with much sorrow, and went away from us, weeping and complaining, into the forest, where she slew herself in the agony of her grief.

"On the morrow, when the troops had moved off a little, we succeeded in getting away further into the jungle..."

The 9th June, 1902, I happened to be with a scouting party, and came upon the body of the dead woman. It was still warm, and a native knife, embedded right up to the hilt, had pierced the heart. Like the rest of my comrades, I imagined at the time that this unfortunate creature had been murdered by the rebels; and it was only several weeks later, when assisting at the examination of the deserter mentioned above, that I learned what had really happened.

On my return to Nha-Nam in May, I had been glad to renew relations with my friend Doy-Tho; and whenever I found time to do so, I passed my evenings in his caigna, and, seated beside him as he smoked, talked over the situation.

He was always very well informed on all that was going on, though he most certainly owed much of his knowledge to his former enemy, but now devoted friend, Linh-Nghi, who, since the termination of the main operations, had been nominated to the important post of lu-thuong (headman) of the village of Long-Thuong; and, in return for the services he had rendered to the authorities, important stretches of cultivated land, formerly owned by some of the rebels, had been made over to him.

It was from Tho that I learned of the lasting impression which the rapid capture of all De-Tam's fortifications had produced upon the population of the Yen-Thé. The majority of the people, he said, were no longer moved to enthusiasm by this chiefs appeals to their patriotism, and they now possessed no confidence in the ultimate success of the movement in favour of their exiled monarch. However, my friend was never weary of repeating that, until the French succeeded in killing or capturing De-Tam, the chief would be a source of constant trouble in the region, because most of the peasants possessed such a real dread of him, that but few of the villages would dare to refuse his demands for money or rice, so long as he remained an outlaw, and had at his disposal a band of cruel and determined partisans.

Though I think that Tho was glad of my company, it was evident to me that he was chagrined at my continued refusal to become a votary of the soothing drug, which, like the majority of his compatriots, he regarded as one of the necessities of existence. His disgust at my persistence was all the more intense because it was an open secret that several of the French officers and sergeants, serving in the native regiments, smoked opium, and took but little pains to conceal the fact. He would give me as examples the names of his superiors who indulged in the pleasure procured by the subtle poison, hoping to induce me to follow their example; though, curiously enough, he would generally conclude his exhortations with quaint reflections full of irony, concerning the excess to which most of the Europeans who indulged in this passion would go; and he would then, in grandiloquent terms, replete with Oriental conceit, inform me that he was himself complete master of his own desires. He would swell with pride and delight when, to humour him, I would praise his powers of self-control, though, for the matter of that, I was convinced the length of his purse and the veto of Ba, his wife, had more to do with the number of pipes he smoked, than any check he was himself capable of imposing on his cravings.

He would speak at length on this subject, bringing out his words with a slow, drawling, sing-song cadence in which there was no indication of emotion, though now and again, when he had given an opinion he considered was possessed of more than ordinary value, he would pause somewhat longer than necessary, watching me intently the while, to see if I had fully grasped the sense of his argument and appreciated the beauty of his flowery metaphor.

"Yes, friend," he would say. "Tell me, I beg you, has not Heaven given to us men the different pleasures of life so that we shall draw from them delight wherewith to lighten our troubles and to forget our hardships? Indeed you do know, since I myself told it to you, that our wise men have long since decided that these numerous and varied pleasures can be classified according to their merits, which consist in the degree of bliss they can procure us. Each of these emotions finds its proper place in its proper section, which last is itself one of 'The Seven Joys,' even as a soldier has his appointed position in one of the four battalions of his regiment. The ancients represented 'The Seven Joys' by as many bats, because, like our pleasures, these animals flit around us in eccentric curves; though it requires but a little patience and a light blow to bring them to our feet. That is why in our pagodas, our houses and upon the altars to our ancestors you will always see, sculptured or painted, the seven bats which are 'The Seven Joys.'

"Heaven has sent us a thousand flowers—of which the most beautiful is the sacred lotus—so that we should admire their colours and shape, glory in their scent and draw great joy therefrom; also the splendour of our hills, our forests and our rivers, the beauty of our women, the love of our little ones, the pleasures of the chase, and the gladness in the slaughter of our foes, are only a few of the million joys in life, amongst which Ong-Tu-phian (Lord Opium) is not the least in importance; and these blessings have been generously accorded us by the Lord Buddha himself, and any refusal to participate in them is indeed rank blasphemy. But be warned that in all things there must be moderation, and because of our friendship, I would not see you do like the Ong-Quan-hai (lieutenant) I have already spoken of, for, if his orderly speaks not lies, this young man smokes one hundred and twenty pipes each day, which is a great foolishness indeed; for in this way his pleasure is no longer his servant, to come and go at his bidding, but rather he has become the slave of his pleasure. Neither is his case an exception, for nearly all you Western foreigners are alike in this matter, and ever you go to the extremes. Either you will not touch the drug—most probably because you are afraid of yourselves—or, if you once begin, you will increase each day the number of pipes you smoke, until your pleasure kills you, instead of remaining content with a moderate use of it."

In speaking thus Tho was but echoing the opinions of his compatriots, for the inhabitants of Indo-China, like the Chinese, are convinced of their superiority, so far as intelligence is concerned, over the European.

Partly from curiosity and also because I was determined to show this little brown man that I possessed more self-restraint than he gave me credit for, I consented one evening to make the experiment, and smoked four pipes. I was rewarded by a most violent headache, prolonged nausea, and a sleepless night crowded with waking nightmare. It is hardly necessary to add that I did not repeat the experiment; and though for some time Tho persisted in telling me that I had not given the drug a fair trial, he finally dropped the subject. But it is probable that my inability to partake of his favourite pleasure was to him another proof of the decided inferiority of the European.

About the middle of June, Lieutenant Deleuze, the intelligence officer from Thaï-Nguyen, to whom reference was made in a preceding chapter, came to us to assist in the operations that were going on, for owing to his knowledge of the vernacular, of the natives and their customs, he was able to obtain information when others, less gifted, would most certainly have failed. This officer was also instructed to complete a new map of the region, for the late expedition had brought to light the many errors and omissions contained in the former surveys of the province. My friend Lipthay accompanied the Lieutenant, for he was to assist in the topographical work.

I was pleased, indeed, to see my friend again, and was happy at being able to congratulate him on his recent promotion, for he was now a corporal; and we "wetted his stripes" on the evening of his arrival with several bottles of good wine. In confidence he informed me that I was myself to be attached to the intelligence staff of the district; and, though he disclaimed all knowledge of the cause, I soon found out that I owed this chance of promotion to his good offices.

I little knew at the time what important changes in my existence this new departure would bring me, though had I possessed that knowledge it could hardly have increased my gratitude for the "good turn" my chum had done me.

For a month I worked with Lieutenant Deleuze, and accompanied the different reconnaissances and little columns; making rough surveys of the ground covered, and bringing back the sketches to Nha-Nam, where they were amplified and checked. During these expeditions I was mounted on a native pony, and armed with a carbine instead of the longer and less handy rifle.

My new life was a most agreeable one, for not only did I escape all the drudgery of fatigue duties in the fort, but when the reconnaissance with which I might happen to be out, got in touch with the enemy, I would put away my compass and planchette and do duty as a galloper; carrying information from the scouts to the commanding officer, and going back again with orders. My mount was only 11½ hands in height, so that when I was in the saddle my feet were but a few inches from the ground, but the animal's pluck, endurance and surefootedness were extraordinary.

On the 15th July, Lipthay, together with the other members of the district staff, returned to Thaï-Nguyen. I was left behind, as my employment had only been a temporary one; but I continued to do topographical work for our Captain, and was in consequence spared the ordinary company routine.

Owing to the extreme heat which had now set in, the authorities gave orders for the suspension of all operations, except in case of great urgency, so that nothing more exciting went on than an occasional hour of drill or theoretical instruction. Having failed to capture De-Tam while it was still possible to move the troops, the authorities were now obliged to wait for cooler weather.

Within the réduit, or little citadel, of our fort, a military telegraph office had been erected, communicating with Bo-Ha and Thaï-Nguyen by wire, and with Mo-Trang and Mona-Luong by the heliograph. Two French operators, a marine and a gunner, were in charge of the station.

Since I had been detached on special service I had messed with these two telegraphists, and it was not long before we were the best of friends. Bougand, the marine, and Gremaire, the gunner, were Parisians of good family and education; and, thanks to their natural versatility and wit, we soon found means of introducing a certain amount of fun into our existence, which helped to relieve the terrible monotony of life in the fort.

By nailing a damp sheet over a window which gave upon the gun-platform, and with the aid of a powerful lamp, sometimes used for signalling at night, we started a shadow theatre. Our troupe and scenery we cut out of thick cardboard, and we were able to present adaptations of some of the most popular dramas and comedies of the day, the text and mise-en-scène of which would have been a startling revelation to the original authors.

These performances were given twice a week, and lasted from 7.30 till 9 p.m., and our audience was composed of all the Legionaries not on duty and such of the native troops as cared to attend. There was, of course, no accommodation for the spectators, who were indeed above such details; and they contented themselves with standing, or squatting, upon the hard ground to watch the show. Though some of our audience saw fit to make rude remarks concerning the tone of voice in which the feminine rôles were read, the majority were unsparing of their applause; and the appearance of the silhouettes of such famous artists as the golden-voiced Sarah or the two Coquelins brought down the house. Now and again some ready-witted interruption from one of the spectators would cause the temporary disappearance of the actors from the stage and a momentary cessation of the performance, for, unable to control our emotions or continue the dialogue, we would fall on the floor of the little mat-shed hut, where we would lie convulsed with laughter, until the noisy public threatened to pull down the house unless we continued the play.

Success ofttimes breeds foolhardiness, and in an evil hour, finding that we had exhausted the répertoire our memories offered us, of plots from the Parisian stage, we decided to draw on local incidents for the construction of our plays. At first all went well, for such farces as The De-Tam's Defeat, in which that chief, after refusing the hand of the Governor-General's daughter and a big dowry, died through incautiously tasting the contents of a tin of bully-beef, supplied by the Commissariat for the use of the troops, were successful, and produced no untoward results. But, craving for still greater popularity, we were foolish enough to put upon our stage the too transparently caricatured counterpart of one of the senior non-commissioned officers in the company of native troops, who, though an excellent soldier, was possessed of many eccentricities. This veteran resented our impudence, and we were reported and obliged to suspend our performances.

The instruments were placed in the upper storey of the little telegraph station, and I was in the habit of sitting upstairs for a couple of hours each evening with either of my friends who happened to be on duty. Here we would chat and smoke—for the messages were few and far between after eight—and while away the time till eleven.

On the evening of 22nd May I was there as usual; Bougand was on duty, and we had been exchanging opinions concerning the adjutant, who had succeeded in obtaining the clôture of our theatre, when our conversation was suddenly interrupted by a call on the Morse from Thaï-Nguyen. In the middle of the message he was receiving, my companion gave a sudden whoop of astonishment; though this did not cause me much emotion, for I was accustomed by now to his pet mania, which consisted in telling me all sorts of tall stories concerning the wires he received, and I prepared myself to greet a yarn about the capture of De-Tam, or my promotion to the much-desired dignity of a full blown corporal. When the message was finished, and he had rapped back that he had read the same correctly, he jumped up excitedly, came over to me and, holding out his hand, shouted:

"Mon vieux, I congratulate you!"

"Blagueur!" I answered. "Spare me your mouldy joke. It's much too hot to laugh, so be sensible. Let's take a glass of wine, if any remains in the bottle, and then I'll go to bed."

"I assure you——" He almost yelled it, but I would not let him go on, and taunted him with the staleness of the joke he was trying to play; till, in despair of obtaining a hearing, he rushed over to the instrument, tore off the band and handed it to me to read. To my amazement I saw, clearly printed in little blue letters upon the narrow strip of paper, beyond the possibility of a hoax, the following message:

"Major—Thaï-Nguyen, to Captain-Commanding Nha-Nam.—Send soldier Manington by first convoy to Phulang-Thuong, from whence he will proceed to Bac-Ninh to take service as secretary, Brigade Staff."

The next few minutes were exciting ones, and it was not until we had hauled Gremaire from his bed downstairs, communicated the news to him, and drowned our emotion in a jugful of wine and water, with a lemon cut up in it, that things began to assume their normal proportions.

I slept but little that night, and lay speculating as to how it was that fortune had so favoured me, for a berth on the Staff meant interesting work, extra pay and comfortable quarters; in fact, a return to partial civilisation. The change carried with it one drawback, however, which made me hesitate as to whether it would not be better for me to propose another man in my place, for I knew that promotion was very slow on the Brigade, the number of "non-coms" there being limited to three, and I was already somewhat disappointed at not receiving my "stripes" at the same time as my friend Lipthay; though this had been owing to the fact that several corporals had been sent out to the corps with the last batch of troops from Algeria, so that the vacancies had been few, and only the best had been chosen.

Next morning I was called up to the rapport, and after Captain Watrin had informed me of the order received from our Major, I told him of my fears; but he would not listen to them at length, and informed me that I must go: that he was proud that a man from his company had been chosen, and that I might congratulate myself on my good luck.

"Why, mon garçon," he said, "you have only to do your work well and keep sober—and you will do that, I know, for the honour of the company—and promotion will come in good time. In two years you will probably be a sergeant; and then, if you so choose, you will be able to go to St Maixent (the military school for sergeants who wish to become officers), and get a commission. Now go to the sergeant-major and get your feuille de route, for you will leave with the convoy to Bo-Ha to-morrow morning." Then, offering me his hand, this excellent man and true gentleman said: "Now, good luck to you; and be careful to remember always that you belong to the Legion, and that the honour of the corps is yours also."

After packing my kit and getting my papers from the sergeant-major, who chaffed me good-naturedly by saying that now that I was going to be on intimate terms with a general, he hoped I would not put on too much "side," I went round the company to say good-bye. Later I slipped away to Tho's hut in the native village, and told him of my coming departure. The little man was evidently chagrined at the news; nevertheless, he congratulated me most heartily, and made me promise to write to him, saying, with evident pride, that he was now able to read a little French, so that, with the aid of one of the native clerks in the Commissariat Department, he would be able to decipher my letters.

We had a grand dinner that evening in the little telegraph station, a tin of salmon and several bottles of beer having been purchased to swell the menu provided by our usual rations.

My friends drank to my success, and I to their health and speedy return to France; and it was late in the night before I retired to rest for the last time in the fort which had, with few intervals, been my home for the past fifteen months.

Several of my comrades were present to bid me "Godspeed" when, early the next morning, I filed out with the convoy through the gates of our position.

Together with several sick men, both Legionaries and tirailleurs, who were going down to the hospital, I left Bo-Ha that evening. We descended the river in sampans, and reached Phulang-Thuong next morning.

On the morning of the 26th July I left for Bac-Ninh with the weekly convoy to Hanoï which carried the mails. We passed through Dap-Cau at noon, and arrived at our destination at 2 p.m. The country we traversed was a big cultivated plain, dotted with villages, with here and there occasional small groups of low hills.

At Bac-Ninh there is a small citadel, built, no doubt, towards the end of the eighteenth century by one of the engineers lent by Louis XVI. to his ally, the Emperor of Annam. It is hexagonal in shape, and constructed according to the principles of Vauban. Each of its sides has a frontage of about 1000 yards, and is furnished with numerous flanking bastions and demi-lunes. There was a company of marines, a battalion of the 3rd Regiment of Tirailleurs Tonkinois, and about a thousand militia in garrison there. Inside the citadel were the houses of the General Commanding the 2nd Brigade, the Resident of the province, the officers' quarters, the barracks of the troops, the Staff offices, and the lodgings of the soldier-secretary.

On my arrival I reported to the Brigade Major, Captain Michaud, who sent me on with an orderly to the Intelligence Department, where I was to be employed.

The chief of this office, Lieutenant Cassier, received me very kindly; and, after telling one of the secretaries, a marine, to go and show me where our lodgings were situated, he informed me that I might rest that afternoon, and come to work the next morning.

I found that I was quartered, together with the other scribes—five privates and two corporals—in a one-roomed brick building with a verandah in front, which was situated at the end of the General's garden, and looked out into the parade ground of the native infantry. On the other side of this open space, about 300 yards away, were the buildings occupied by the French marines.

I washed, disposed my kit above the cot which I noted was of the comfortable pattern in use in Algeria, and went for a stroll into the town, about a couple of hundred yards outside the fortifications, for I desired to reconnoitre the surroundings before dinner, which I had been informed was at 6 p.m.

The little town of Bac-Ninh is situated on the old mandarin road from Hanoï (the capital of Tonquin) to Lang-son and the Chinese frontier, about 18 miles from the metropolis. It contains a population of eight thousand natives, is the capital of the province of the same name, and has a cathedral, seat of the Spanish bishopric of eastern Tonquin. Though it is not a manufacturing centre of any importance, its only local production being silk embroidery work—for which, however, it is famous—it is considered as one of the principal commercial towns of the colony, because its markets are a medium of barter or exchange for objects imported from the surrounding provinces and also from China, through the frontier towns of Lang-son and Cao-Bang. I wandered through the narrow streets for an hour or so, and was delighted with the life and bustle of the little town. It was market day, and the busy throngs jostled one another as they passed to and fro. The natives are noisy individuals, and their shrill cries as they hawked their wares or wrangled over the price of some article for household use—a basket of rice, yams, or some other comestible—were perfectly bewildering at first to me; for I had become so used to the silence of the empty plains and the jungle-covered hills, that even the tiny stir of this overgrown village produced an impression akin to what an inhabitant of Exmoor might feel were he suddenly transported to the busiest centre of London.

I got back in good time to the citadel, for I was anxious not to commit so serious a breach of etiquette as to make my new comrades await dinner for me.

I received a hearty welcome from them all, though only one of them, a lance-corporal, who was working in the general office, belonged to the Legion: he came from the 2nd Regiment. We sat down to our meal in a small building close to the offices of the Brigade; and the fare, which was better than I had been used to at Nha-Nam, and the unexpected luxuries of china plates, real glasses, a table covered with white oil-cloth and a punkah, were more than sufficient to reconcile me to my new surroundings. Owing to the extra pay we drew—about one and sixpence a day—it was not only possible to keep up a good mess, but, besides the cook, we were able to maintain a boy, at four piastres a month—about eight shillings—and this faithful servitor swept out our quarters, made the beds, cleaned our boots, pipe-clayed our helmets, and performed a hundred and one other services, which I had become so used to doing for myself that it was several days before I could become accustomed to leave the work to him, much to the amusement of the other secretaries.

The morning after my arrival I rose and dressed at 5.30 a.m., as I had been used to do in my company; but I got roundly sworn at by the other occupants of the room for awakening them by my noisy ablutions. The fault lay with them, however, for they had neglected to inform me that the office opened at eight, though it was several weeks before I could accustom myself to lie abed till seven each morning.

I found that my task consisted partly in aiding in the drawing up of a new map of the Yen-Thé, and partly in clerical and intelligence work. This last part was the most interesting, for I had to write down the reports of the different spies attached to the Brigade, and the depositions of the captured brigands when they were interrogated by the lieutenant in charge of our office. Besides this, I had to pass an hour each morning with the Brigade Major, as it was my duty to register all the correspondence received, the letters and reports being handed over to me for that purpose by Captain Michaud, as soon as he had perused them. By this means I became acquainted with everything of interest that was going on in the colony, so far as rebellion, brigandage and military operations were concerned; and I had not been long on the staff before I realised that the little warfare in which my company had taken a part in the Yen-Thé was but a chapter in the history of a struggle that was still going on all over the country, outside of the Delta provinces, between the French on one hand and the Tonquinese rebels and Chinese bands on the other. Columns were marching, or being organised, against such chiefs as Luu-Ky, whose powerful gangs of well-armed plunderers overran the provinces of Quang-Yen, Lam and Lang-son; the veteran banditti of the quasi-feudal lords, Ba-Ky and Luong-Tam-Ky, in the districts of Cao-Bang and Ha-Giang, on the higher reaches of the Red River, and the frontiers of Yunan, Kwang-si and Kwang-tung; and skirmishes were reported daily by the officers who commanded the numerous forts and blockhouses, whose garrisons were continually coming in touch with the bands infesting the mountainous regions of the colony.

CHAPTER VIII

    Time dealt gently with the able officer who was in command of the 2nd Brigade at Bac-Ninh in 1892; for this General, when at the head of the French corps, serving ten years later with the allied army under Marschall Waldersee in China, was still the same thick-set, active soldier, whose rugged features bespoke the energy and determination of the man, and whose eyes held the genial light which did not belie the kindly nature of the soul within. Throughout the whole of his long career this officer was associated with France's colonial army. As a young officer he was severely wounded at the defence of Bazeille in 1870. He served afterwards under Faidherbe in the Soudan and Senegal, and with Brière de l'Isle in Tonquin.

    The man-in-the-ranks of all armies is never at a loss to find an appropriate nickname for a superior who appeals to his regard or dislike, and this General had not been long in command before he became known to the men, in the French and foreign battalions alike, as "Papa Voyron." It would, indeed, have been difficult to find another cognomen conveying with equal truthfulness the just, firm and fatherly manner in which he treated the troops under his orders.

    It is a pleasure to do justice to the high military capabilities and admirable characteristics of this popular French officer; but it must nevertheless be stated that the speech made by General Voyron at Marseilles, on his return from Pekin in 1902, containing as it did several adverse and unmerited criticisms on the discipline and courage of our Indian troops, was a source of some surprise to me. However, when one takes into consideration that of late years politics have unfortunately occupied a predominant place in the minds of France's most capable military men, and also that public feeling was unfavourable to England at the time this speech was made, it may be assumed that these aspersions, which tally badly with the character of the gallant officer, were but the result of a passing wave of popular sentiment, to the effects of which the Gallic temperament is always so susceptible.

    The Commandant of the Brigade, like many others of his profession, possessed a hobby, as far removed from le métier des armes as the not infrequent desire fostered by many old merchant skippers for keeping a poultry-farm is from the art of navigation. This hobby was horticulture. It should be mentioned that during the cooler months of each year in Tonquin—October to April—all the edible green stuffs of the temperate zones can be grown with success; though to obtain really good results fresh seed must be procured annually from Europe. General Voyron made it his special care that all the stations in the interior where white troops were garrisoned should possess a kitchen-garden. Thanks to this wise measure the men, to the benefit alike of their health and palate, were, and are still, supplied during six months out of twelve with abundant quantities of fresh vegetables; and the quality of the crops obtained from the trim, well-kept gardens is a cause of emulation in each of these small garrisons.

Whenever the General inspected the different forts situated in the regions under his care, he never failed to look round these gardens; and, when they showed proof that care had been bestowed upon them, he was lavish in his expressions of satisfaction; but there would be a mauvais moment à passer for the unfortunate officer who had neglected or ignored the Brigadier's circulars containing recommendations concerning the necessity of ensuring a liberal supply of vegetables for the men.

The internal organisation of the Brigade Staff was very simple. There were three departments, the first being the general office, the staff of which was charged with the elucidation of all questions relating to administration, promotion and discipline in the corps belonging to the Brigade, the printing and despatching of general orders and circulars, and the drawing up of the monthly reports concerning the available effectives, the existing stocks of arms and ammunition, and the general health of the troops.

The Intelligence Department was the second section, and the duties of its chief were both numerous and delicate, some of the most important being the control of the surveying and topographical bureau, the interrogation of spies or prisoners, and administration of the Secret Service funds, the translation of code telegrams, the classification of the documents relative to the active operations of the Brigade, and the editing of the monthly confidential reports concerning the existing bands of rebels and brigands, which gave detailed information as to their organisation, approximate strength, armament and zones of action.

The third department was the office of the Brigade Major, through which all completed work passed for inspection and annotation before being transmitted to the General for signature, and from which the first two sections received instructions.

The Chief of the Staff, who was at the head of this office, was also charged with the transmission of the General's decisions, relative to punishments or censure inflicted on officers under his orders; and to his care were entrusted the confidential notes concerning each of these subordinates. These notes consisted of information concerning the past services, punishments, special aptitudes or failings, as the case might be, of each officer in the Brigade, and were contained in a little parchment-covered book known as the livret individuel, on the outside of which was written the name of the person it concerned. One such book is made out for every sub-lieutenant as soon as he passes out of St Cyr and obtains his commission, and this little tell-tale record follows him from corps to corps during the whole of his career. It will be easily understood that it is considered a matter of extreme importance that no officer should ever become acquainted with the contents of his livret individuel, and to this effect the only persons who are allowed to handle them are the commandant of his regiment, who notes therein every six months his appreciations of his subordinate's military capabilities and moral conduct, the Chief of the Brigade Staff and the General.

The Secretaries on the Brigade took turns on night duty, for it was necessary that a man should be at the office from 6 p.m. to 6 a.m. to receive the telegrams when they arrived, and, in event of their being of urgent importance, to send them on to the Chief of the Staff. We were so busy in the Intelligence Department that in the first week in September the Major decided to get another man, so as to relieve me and aid in the topographical work. To my delight Lipthay was chosen for the post, so that a few days later I was able to welcome my old chum into his new quarters. This increase in work was due to the state of affairs on the railway then in construction from Phu-lang-Thuong to Lang-son, for the region was overrun by bands of Chinese brigands, under the orders of the famous Luu-Ky, who attacked the working parties, and carried away into captivity several of the French engineers and contractors. Encouraged by their success, the robbers ambuscaded several of the convoys going by road to Lang-son, and, after slaying the majority of the escort, carried off important quantities of treasure, several cases of Lebel rifles and a good deal of ammunition. In one of these engagements a major of the Infanterie de Marine, Commandant Bonneau, was shot dead. So great was the mobility of these bands, and such excellent cover was offered by the mountainous country on either side of the road, that all attempts to engage and scatter them, made by the little parties of troops garrisoned in the different forts, proved of no avail; and it soon became evident that it would require a strong and well-organised column to secure any favourable results, to ensure the security of the route, and to allow of the work upon the railway being continued. In August General Reste, the Commander-in-Chief at Hanoï, made an urgent appeal to the Governor-General for permission to undertake operations against Luu-Ky, on a scale to ensure success; but M. de Lanessan refused to countenance any such movement, and declared that the military authorities ought to be able to crush the bands with the forces already at their disposal, in garrison along the Lang-son route. There is little doubt that the Governor in making this reply was influenced by political motives. The recent successful operations in the Yen-Thé had been utilised to further his political aspirations in France, and the metropolitan press had repeatedly announced, with a great flourish of trumpets, that rebellion and brigandage were now dead in Tonquin. Indeed, in one of his reports to the Colonial Minister, M. de Lanessan had declared that, owing to the success of his administration, the pacification of the colony was now an assured fact, and it was possible to wander over the country with no other protection than a stout walking-stick. The absurdity of such statements was clear in Tonquin, but they found favour with the public in France, where people were only too willing to believe that an era of peace and plenty was at last to open in their Far Eastern possessions, with a consequent cessation of the enormous sacrifices of men and money that had accompanied the past ten years. The Governor, because of this advertisement, was declared to be the first of France's Viceroys capable of grappling with the situation; and as it was his firm intention to again contest, in the near future, the seat in the Chamber which he had resigned on accepting the high position he was now filling, he can hardly be blamed, in a country where men take up politics as a business, for fostering interests which would assure him a considerable number of votes when the time came. That this state of affairs was detrimental to the progress of the colony is certain, but political influence, party hatred and electioneering jobbery have had much to do with retarding the development of Indo-China, since its administration was placed in the hands of a civilian governor and staff in 1886.

It is, however, possible that the Governor made these declarations in good faith, for he had hardly been a year in the country, and was obliged to rely for advice on the Residents and Vice-Residents; and these civilians, hating the military element, were only too eager to throw doubts on the exactitude of the information contained in the reports coming in from the military territories, and they openly declared that the officers of the colonial army were intentionally exaggerating the gravity of the situation in the hope of provoking operations likely to bring them promotion and decorations. The contradictory advice of his civilian staff was possibly one of the causes which led the Governor to pooh-pooh the importance of this new upheaval, declaring that the Generals were alarmists, and that the well-armed and organised bands of Luu-Ky were "que des voleurs de vaches pour venir au bout desquels il suffirait de quelques gendarmes" ("only cattle-stealers with whom a few policemen could deal"). These declarations provoked the anger and disgust of every officer and man in the colony, and very soon a veritable hatred reigned between the civil and military elements. The different newspapers sided with the parties appealing most to their sentiments or their pockets; for it was an open secret that some of these journals were subventioned by the Government, and a wordy warfare wherein neither insults nor invective were spared, was the order of the day. Doubtless there were faults on both sides; and it is certain that the Commander-in-Chief committed an unpardonable error by issuing general orders to the troops, to be read at parades and posted up in the barracks, in which the civilian authorities were belittled and reproached with having insulted the army. This necessarily added fuel to the fire; and the situation became so strained that officers and civilians came to fisticuffs in the streets of the capital, and several serious duels took place.

Things were, however, brought to a climax towards the end of August by the abduction of three Frenchmen on the railway-line, one of whom, M. Vezin, was the principal engineer representing the big contracting firm, Fives-Lille & Co. The consternation in high quarters when this news was received was considerable, for there existed no possible chance of keeping such thrilling information out of the newspapers in Paris.

As soon as the coup had been successfully carried through, Luu-Ky retired into the security of his lair in the mountains of the Bao-Day range, and from here he sent out messengers to the nearest military station, announcing that he would release the prisoners on the receipt of a sum of $100,000 in silver; but he also declared that, in event of the troops approaching his encampment he would have the captives executed immediately. The excitement throughout the colony was intense, and party rancour was forgotten in the general anxiety felt for the three unfortunate prisoners, as the cruelty of the Chinese bandits was well known to all. After three weeks of negotiation a slight reduction in the ransom was obtained, and the three gentlemen were released, after having suffered indignity and torture at the hands of their captors, with the result that their constitutions were wrecked by privation and exposure.

The Governor still refused, however, to authorise effective operations against the robbers; and it was not until several military convoys had been captured, and a good many officers and men slain, that M. de Lanessan finally agreed that the bandits were worthy of more serious attention than they had previously received. When the column actually commenced operations its work was considerably facilitated by the death of the famous chief Luu-Ky, from the effects of a wound received during the attack made on the convoy when Major Bonneau was killed; but, owing to the rugged nature of the country in which the operations took place, it was fully six weeks before the brigands were defeated and scattered. A good many of the bandits escaped into Kwang-si, and others fled to the mountainous regions in the north.

The telegrams and reports, coming in from the column, were of great interest to me, as my company was taking part in the battue. I happened to be on night duty one evening towards the end of September, when a wire was received stating that a detachment of my comrades had been caught in an ambuscade, among the rocky defiles of the Kai-Kinh, at a point not far from Cho-Trang, my former garrison. This despatch mentioned that Captain Watrin, our commander, was among the slain. Both Lipthay and myself were shocked at this news. We experienced, however, a certain relief on hearing next day that the body of our chief had not fallen into the hands of the enemy, though seven of the men were hit while carrying the corpse out of a narrow defile to a place of safety.

Several months later I met a man who had assisted at this engagement, and he informed me that the Legionaries went raving mad when they learned that this popular officer was killed, and, after rushing the position—to gain which they had to pass, one at a time, down a sort of narrow funnel, 50 feet long, swept by the enemy's fire—they slew every Chinaman found behind the improvised ramparts. Our losses were very heavy, owing to the strength of the position, but the men would not be denied, and took a terrible revenge for the death of their Captain. In October the rebel chief began to give trouble again. He made overtures for peace, and, profiting by the confidence thus inspired, and the absence of the majority of the troops from the region, he left his retreat in the forest, and captured and occupied a strongly-fortified village called Ban-Cuc, about 10 miles south of Nha-Nam. He established his headquarters there, and ravaged the surrounding district, until, a fortnight later, he was driven from his fastness by a column under Major Barr, and again escaped to the mountains with the majority of his men.

Notwithstanding the hard work we were having on the Brigade, time passed agreeably at Bac-Ninh, for there was plenty to see in the town when we were off duty—that is, for any one interested in studying the native industries and customs. Besides, to relieve the monotony of garrison life, the General had encouraged the French troops to organise a theatrical troupe, which gave some very amusing concerts and dramatic performances in a temporary theatre in the barracks, the Commandant of the Brigade and his staff never failing to attend. In October General Reste was recalled to France, and General Duchemin took over the supreme command of the troops in the colony, after which the animosity between the civilians and military subsided.

At this time I was often left in charge of the Intelligence Department, for Lieutenant Cassier and Lipthay were away three days in each week, making a new survey of the surrounding country. During one of these outings they were approached by the headman of a village, who begged them to come and slay a man-eating tiger that had established his headquarters in a cluster of trees inside the hamlet itself. The beast had been there three days already, and each morning had seized upon and devoured one of the unfortunate inhabitants, so that the remainder were afraid to leave their houses. The natives declared that they had employed every available means of driving the fierce brute away, but the beating of drums and gongs, the throwing of lances and lighted torches into the scrub, had only served to enrage their uninvited guest, and that very morning one of the villagers who had approached too near to the thicket, had been slain before the eyes of his comrades. The officer and my friend, taking with them their escort, consisting of ten native soldiers and a corporal, proceeded at once to the scene of the tragedy. The tirailleurs, instructed to shout and keep on firing off their rifles in the air from time to time, were told to advance upon the little clump of trees from three sides at once, while the lieutenant and Lipthay waited on the other. By these means they succeeded in driving the tiger out into the open, and he was despatched with a couple of well-aimed shots. I saw the beast when brought into Bac-Ninh; he was a fine specimen of his kind, measuring 9 feet 7 inches from the tip of the tail to the muzzle.

At this period of my service I was promoted to the post of archiviste, and thus was placed in charge of all the records of the Brigade. I should mention that at this time they were in a serious state of disorder, owing to the negligence of the secretary who had preceded me in this work; so that I was obliged to set to and sort the whole of them. It was somewhat weary work at first, wading through this mass of paper: the greater part consisting of musty, dust-covered dossiers, dating back, some of them, to the conquest of the country by the French. But there were documents of immense interest among this medley of yellow, evil-smelling and worm-eaten despatches; and the reconstruction, with the aid of all the original reports of the famous march of General de Négrier to Lang-son and the frontier of China, the subsequent retreat to Kep, and the enquiry prior to the court-martial held on the unfortunate Colonel Herbinger, who took over the command of the troops after the General was wounded at Ky-Lua, was a source of pure joy to me for several days.

In December General Voyron left Tonquin for France, and Colonel Gallieni, later a General and Governor of Madagascar, came down from Lang-son, where he was in command of the 1st Military Territory, and took over the service par interim. The Governor-General, who had already done away with the brigade at Son-Tay, thinking, no doubt, that this was a magnificent occasion to weaken still further the hand of the military party in the colony, decided to dispense with another brigadier, so he issued a decree abolishing the command at Bac-Ninh. Probably the fact that the announcement of this step would be hailed in France as another proof of the supposed pacification of the country was an inducement to the taking of this measure.

It is doubtful, from a military standpoint, if the change was a wise one; for, though it saved the colony about £4,800 a year—the salary of two generals—it was hardly possible for the Commander-in-Chief in Hanoï to deal directly with the commandants of the different regiments, military territories and garrisons in the Delta, who were scattered all over so vast a country. Indeed, the insufficiency of the new system was so evident that the authorities eventually returned to the original arrangement; and to-day, though the country is almost completely pacified, there exist two brigades in Tonquin and one in Cochin-China.

However, though M. de Lanessan planned this important change in the colony, the Colonial Ministry in Paris did not look at affairs in the same light. As soon as they learned that General Voyron was leaving, they sent out General Pernot to replace him, and the latter arrived in Indo-China to find that the post he had come out to fill, no longer existed.

M. de Lanessan would have liked to send the General back to France—and indeed he proposed to do so—but the authorities in Paris, probably because they had no post for the officer at home, insisted that he should remain. Thus the brigade was resuscitated for his benefit, and its secretaries, already on their way to rejoin their respective regiments, were recalled to Bac-Ninh. I had been in Phulang-Thuong four days, and was awaiting a convoy for Nha-Nam, when the order arrived for my return, and its arrival caused me no little surprise and speculation.

Two days later I was back in my old place, my absence having lasted about a week, and the following morning General Pernot came up from Hanoï with his staff.

He was a short, fat, red-faced man with a very loud, disagreeable voice, and a temper that was worse; and his reputation with the men of being a crusty martinet was not altogether unjustified. The day following his arrival he came to the office and passed a review of the secretaries. On learning that I was in charge of the records, he came over to where I was standing at "attention," and asked:

"You are naturalised, I suppose?"

"No, mon Général," I answered.

"What! not naturalised yet! You have the intention of becoming so, of course?"

"No, mon Général," I replied.

He glared up at me with an angry stare, and his face took a dull-red colour. I thought he was going to burst.

"Oh, indeed!" he blurted out at last. "You must put in an application to become a French citizen, or go back to your battalion. I will have no foreigners in a post of confidence on my staff. Grand Dieu! what have they been doing to allow such a thing? It is shameful! Nom de nom!"

He almost shouted the last words, so great was his indignation, and from the expression he put into them one might have been justified in imagining that the Republic was in danger owing to my presence there. I did not become naturalised, and I heard nothing more about the question; and in justice to this cantankerous officer, I must acknowledge that, during the fifteen months he commanded the Brigade, he treated me with consideration on the rare occasions that I had any direct business to transact with him. He had risen from the ranks—indeed, I was told that he began his career as a sailor on a man-of-war—and it is therefore probable that his modest origin and the hard times he experienced at his début accounted for his rough and rude manners.

Our new Brigade Major, Captain Bataille, was a quiet and reserved gentleman, who studied hard at his profession and was a most capable officer, having already brilliantly distinguished himself in the field, for which he had been decorated with the cross of the Legion of Honour.

We had now no Intelligence Department; and all questions formerly dealt with by this branch, together with those relating to active operations by the troops, were treated by the Headquarters Staff at Hanoï.

The Governor had not succeeded in doing away with the Brigade, but he had taken his revenge by reducing its importance to a minimum, and the rôle of its chief now consisted almost entirely in looking after the details of administration and discipline of the regiments under his orders, and in conducting the annual inspection of the troops in French Indo-China. In January, 1893, we received orders to transfer our offices to Hanoï, and we had rather a lively time of it for several days packing up the records and stowing them away, together with all the portable furniture, into a long string of commissariat mule-carts. Our march to Hanoï was not a fatiguing one, for the distance is not great—about 20 miles—and the road is probably the best in Tonquin.

Owing to the numerous carts we were escorting our progress was not as rapid as it might have been, and it was late in the evening when we reached a point on the left bank of the Red River, just opposite the capital. The country we had traversed during the day was perfectly flat and covered with paddy fields, and I do not think we saw the smallest patch that was not cultivated. The weather was bitterly cold, the mercury having descended almost to freezing point (the winter of '92-'93 was a record one in the colony), and thrice along the route we came upon the bodies of natives who had died from exposure. Our convoy was transported over the stream—nearly a mile wide at this point—by a steam ferry. The accommodation on this ferry was so restricted that only two carts could be taken at a time, so that it was quite dark when we reached the citadel, situated some distance from the landing-stage.

Our new offices were inside the fortress—a fine place, constructed on the same plan as that of Bac-Ninh, the difference between the two being that the superficial area of the first was twice that of the second. These fortifications, first captured by the French in 1872, no longer exist, and on the former site of their ramparts and ditches can now be seen one of the finest quarters of the European town.

Hanoï, the capital of Tonquin, was important and imposing when I first saw it in 1893; and to-day, thanks to the enterprise and good taste of its municipal council, it is certainly one of the finest cities in the Far East. Its rapid development and flourishing condition leads one to reflect on what the colony itself might be were its destinies placed, like those of the metropolis, in the hands of a representative chamber of colonists elected by their fellow-citizens, instead of being entrusted to an army of political functionaries. The city was founded in 865 A.D. by the Emperor Cao-bien, and its original name was Dai-la-Thanh. A succeeding monarch, Thay-Son, constructed a palace there in 1028. Hanoï is admirably situated for commercial purposes, being at the extreme northern limit of the Delta provinces, at a point on the river, 82 miles from Haïphong, where communication with lower Tonquin, by means of the numerous estuaries and canals, is easy and rapid. The same may be said with regard to upper Tonquin and Yunan, which can be reached by the Song-Koï itself. The Dutch merchants established factories or trading posts here, and at Hung-Yen, Nam-Dinh and Haïphong, towards the end of the sixteenth century.

Hanoï has the form of an isosceles triangle, the base of which extends along the river bank for about 2 miles. The inhabitants of the capital owe a good deal to M. de Lanessan, who was the first to suggest the demolition of the immense and useless citadel, which, owing to its situation, retarded the growth of the city northwards. The native quarter of the town is extremely picturesque, and the neat whitewashed houses, not two of which are alike in size or height, with their quaintly-curved, red-tiled roofs, and step-like cornices, the numerous pagodas ornamented with dragons, griffins and genii, produce a vista of pleasant aspect and great interest to the European. There are hundreds of small shops, wherein the natives squat on a piece of matting, surrounded by their wares. Workmen of a like craft, merchants in similar lines of business, flock together and live in the same quarter, so that the majority of the streets in the Annamese portion of the town are named after the objects made or for sale there. Thus it is that one sees at the corners of the thoroughfares such indications as "Bamboo Matting Street," "Hat Street," "Fan Street," "Copper Street," etc., etc. The main arteries of this quarter present a crowded appearance, and traffic is continual, but, contrary to the usual state of affairs in most Oriental cities, the streets are clean and odourless, a fact which can be attributed to an excellent system of police supervision.

The riksha is the favourite means of transportation, although an admirable system of electric tramways has now been started. The native inhabitants of the town dress somewhat more carefully than their fellow-countrymen in the villages; that is to say, the merchants and shopkeepers do so. They all wear the big hat made of palm leaves; and the wealthier classes embellish its appearance by applying a light brown varnish to its exterior and surmounting its crest with a cap of silver scroll-work and a small spike of the same metal.

The Asiatic population of Hanoï is very dense, and in 1902 consisted of 100,000 Annamese and 3,500 Celestials. According to the returns, there were 6,110 native houses in the city, covering a total area of about 165 acres.

The French may well be proud of the European quarter of the capital of Tonquin, for its fine, well-laid-out boulevards and streets, handsome public buildings, big shops, comfortable hotels and well-appointed cafés would do honour to the prèfecture towns of Southern France, such as Arles, Avignon, or Montpelier. Though the principal thoroughfares of the town do not present the busy appearance of our Eastern commercial centres, such as Singapore or Hong-Kong, and one does not meet the hurrying throngs that give to these two cities the characteristics of Anglo-Saxon activity, yet the prospect of the Rue Paul Bert, the principal street at Hanoï, at the hour of the aperitif, is extremely pleasing, and reminds one of the Parisian boulevards. In front of the more important cafés the pavement is occupied by the numerous round marble-topped tables so dear to the boulevardier. After five o'clock every evening these terraces are crowded with habitués who, while sipping their iced absinthe, vermouth or bitter, sit enjoying the cool breeze, exchanging the tittle-tattle of the town, discussing the latest departmental or social scandal, or watching the passing carriages—smart little victorias or dog-carts drawn by diminutive, well-groomed ponies, and provided with yellow-skinned coachmen and "tigers," glorious in their neat liveries and top-boots. At this hour the ladies of the colony, whose means permit of this luxury, drive through the town, out to the fine botanical and zoological gardens, and alight at the Kiosque, to enjoy a stroll in the fresh of the evening, and to listen to the band or partake of a cup of tea or an iced sorbet. The male sex is also en evidence at these gatherings and promenades; consequently the toilettes are brilliant and of the latest fashion, and, with a slight flight of fancy, one might imagine oneself back at the Cascade or the Pré Catalan in the Bois de Boulogne. In 1893, as it is to-day, the palace of the Governor-General, the residence of the Commander-in-Chief, and the offices of the Headquarter Staff are situated in a portion of the town known as the Concession—a strip of ground fronting the river, about 1 mile long by 700 yards broad. This small territory was conceded to the French in 1882 by the Emperor of Annam, and, together with the Concession at Haïphong, which was occupied a few years previously, it may be said to represent the first foothold of France in Tonquin.

The public buildings in the Concession are well built, and are surrounded by fine gardens. The town is provided with a splendid system of surface drainage; it is lighted throughout with electricity, and possesses an adequate water supply, which, however, is the cause of some complaint, owing to the fact that the water is pumped from wells situated in the native quarter of the town and close to the river, from which, it is more than probable, there exists a considerable infiltration.

In the centre of the European quarter of Hanoï there is a lake. The borders of this are covered with trees and shrubs and laid out with paths framed in verdure, so that the effect of the whole is charming. There are two small islands on the lake, and on each of these is a small pagoda. On the largest island, which can be reached by a fine native bridge, about 30 yards long, built of ironwood, is a beautiful, though small, specimen of a native temple, known as the pagoda of the isle of Jade, and for the last five hundred years it has been the rendezvous for the literati of the capital. The zoological and botanical garden, to which reference has already been made, is situated in the extreme north-west corner of the city. It is splendidly laid out, and covers several acres of ground. It is here that the "Society" of Hanoï comes to drive or promenade of an evening before dinner; and its fine avenues, flower-beds, groves and lawns compare favourably with the Cinnamon Gardens in Colombo, or the waterfall at Penang. The roads throughout the town are wide and well built, and in this respect, as in the laying out of the streets, and the style of architecture adapted for the government buildings or for private residences, the French are by far our superiors. This is due partly to the naturally artistic taste they possess, and also to the wise regulations adopted by the Public Works Department in the colony, with regard to the construction of new buildings, all plans having to be approved by the Department before a permit to commence building is granted.

In July, 1892, when I had arrived in Bac-Ninh, it seemed, after my protracted stay in the wild regions of the upper Yen-Thé, that at last I had returned to a large town, and the sight of a few scores of brick buildings was, for the first few days, quite a novelty; but when, six months later, I found myself in the capital of Tonquin, it was like getting back to a big European city, and, though we sometimes regretted the charms of our former adventurous existence, both Lipthay and myself soon began to find a new pleasure in the renewed acquaintance with the comforts and distractions of civilisation. We were not as free as we had been at Bac-Ninh, as we were lodged in a room set apart for us, in the barracks of the 9th Regiment of Infanterie de Marine, and were for a few days the pet grievance of the "non-coms" of that corps, who put us on fatigue duty and made us take part in the inspections. This, however, was soon stopped by the Chief of the Staff, and we were allowed to continue the even tenour of our way. There is always a certain amount of jealousy felt for the scribes of the army, and the French sergeants were probably indignant at the thought that we were drawing as much pay as they were, that we were allowed out every night till 10 p.m., and also because we took our meals at the canteen, in a room specially reserved for us. The latter arrangement was adopted to avoid indiscretions, for a few of us were continually and unavoidably in possession of facts it was of absolute importance the majority of the troops should not learn.

For the next twelve months we continued our somewhat uneventful life as staff secretaries within the ancient precincts of the Annamese citadel, the only break in the monotony of our career being my promotion to the grade of corporal, which occurred in November. I had waited a long time for my stripes, and should have had them sooner had I remained with my corps; but till then there had been no vacancy on the staff for a "non-com," so I had nothing to complain of. In February our offices were again moved, this time to the Concession, in a building close to the Headquarters Staff, and we were lodged with the secretaries of that organisation. Since I had come to Hanoï my health had considerably improved; and very soon after my arrival I was no longer troubled with the attacks of malaria, which formerly, at almost regular intervals, used to lay me up for a day, and sometimes more. The change of air was, I suppose, chiefly responsible for the amelioration, and the better food and more comfortable quarters probably helped to mend matters. Life in the capital was very agreeable, though during the summer months the heat was terrible. This is due to the fact that, because of the low situation of the city, the south-west monsoon is little felt there. The French colonials I happened to come in contact with were extremely kind and hospitable, and during my military career I made several acquaintances which ripened into friendships that never failed me during the subsequent years passed in the colony as a civilian. The French settler, be he either planter, merchant, manufacturer or shopkeeper, is one of the hardest workers I have ever seen. He possesses an admirable faith in the rich country he has adopted, and a supreme contempt for his government, which seems to delight in throwing every possible obstacle in the way of private enterprise, and in ever increasing the number of functionaries he has to pay for.

In April, 1894, General Pernot practically reached the age-limit of his rank, and returned to France, his place being taken by General Coronnat. At the time he took over the command he was the youngest Brigadier-General in the French army, having, thanks to the services he had rendered to the Republic, and to his wide knowledge of his profession, attained that rank when most officers in France's forces esteem themselves happy if they are in command of a regiment. This distinguished soldier was by birth a Basque, the son of a modest cooper, who plied his trade in a small and picturesque village situated at the foot of the rugged and majestic Pyrenees; but he was in demeanour, speech and conduct, one of the truest gentlemen it has been my lot to encounter. Tall, and somewhat sparse, fair, with blue piercing eyes, a straight thin nose, a small light-coloured moustache, and a very strong chin. When listening he was reserved, attentive and courteous; when speaking his voice was wonderfully soft for a military man, and as clear as a bell. On first acquaintance he appeared to affect a certain aloofness; but this was only apparent, and was due, most probably, to the erectness of his bearing, and to his habit of speaking but little, and of fixing his eyes on the person who was addressing him, so that, unless they were acquainted with this particularity, he would stare them out of countenance. Having gained a hard-earned scholarship, the General obtained his grade of sub-lieutenant by passing through the military school of St Cyr, instead of being obliged, like many of small means, to work his way up from the ranks.

The work of pacification went on steadily, but it was destined that I should remain at my post on the Brigade, and take no active part in the different expeditions sent against the pirates and rebels in 1894-95. In October, 1894, I lost my friend Lipthay. He died in the military hospital at Hanoï, worn out with fever and debility acquired during our campaigns in Yen-Thé. I was by him almost to the end, and he passed away calm and courageous, like the noble, true-hearted gentleman he had always proved himself to be. He had been promoted to the rank of sergeant, and had been made a Knight of the Dragon of Annam shortly before his death.

On the 27th February, 1895, I was liberated, having completed a period of five years under the French flag. The experience I had gained was invaluable, and I felt no regret for the step I had taken in enlisting. Nevertheless it was with an emotion akin to delight that I hailed my return to the liberties of civilian life. It should, however, be mentioned that I experienced a certain regret at severing my connection with the French army and the Legion.

While serving in that corps I had learned that there were good and brave men outside my own country, and that courage, obedience, self-abnegation and national pride are not the monopoly of any one race.

By living side by side with them, fighting, and ofttimes suffering, in the same cause, I had been taught to like and respect the foreigners. The French, Italian, German, Austrian, or any other European soldier is very much like our own. He has his virtues and his vices; and the stronger his race and national character, the more likely is he to possess a superabundance of the latter.

British interests in Siam and Southern China render the development of the French colonies in the Far East a matter of importance to us. The majority of the foreign products imported into Yunan, via the West River route, or through Tonquin, are of British origin. Our treaty arrangements with France and the good feeling at present existing between the two nations should make it no difficult matter for Frenchmen and Englishmen to agree in the settlement of questions arising out of their trade relations with Kwang-si, Kwang-tung and Yunan.

The recent concessions made by Siam to France have increased the responsibilities of the latter, and it remains for France and Great Britain to develop the commercial resources of Siam and South China.

By the aid of the railway system, agriculture and manufacturing industries are being fostered in the French colonies of the East, and a great future undoubtedly exists for them; but before real success can be obtained Indo-China must be provided with functionaries who are not only able administrators, but who have a knowledge of the language and customs of the country They must be workers with a single aim for the success of the colonies under their administration, and not merely politicians whose personal ambitions colour their perceptions. Then the colonies, wherein I spent the years of which I have written, will have a future of constantly-increasing prosperity before them.

THE END

Printed in Great Britain
by Amazon